KEY CASES

LEGAL SYSTEM

2nd edition
Jacqueline Martin

D1136516

COMPANY

Orders: please contact Bookpoint Ltd, 130 Milton Park, Abingdon, Oxon OX14 4SB.
Telephone: (44) 01235 827720. Fax: (44) 01235 400454. Lines are open from
9.00 – 5.00, Monday to Saturday, with a 24 hour message answering service.
You can also order through our website www.hoddereducation.co.uk

If you have any comments to make about this, or any of our other titles, please send them to
educationenquiries@hodder.co.uk

British Library Cataloguing in Publication Data
A catalogue record for this title is available from the British Library

ISBN 978 1 444 13531 2

First Edition published	2006
This Edition published	2011
Impression number	10 9 8 7 6 5 4 3 2 1
Year	2014 2013 2012 2011

Copyright © 2006, 2011 Jacqueline Martin

Hachette UK's policy is to use papers that are natural, renewable and recyclable products and
made from wood grown in sustainable forests. The logging and manufacturing processes are
expected to conform to the environmental regulations of the country of origin.

Typeset by Transet Limited, Coventry, England.
Printed in Great Britain for Hodder Education, an Hachette UK Company,
338 Euston Road, London NW1 3BH by CPI Cox & Wyman Ltd, Reading, RG1 8EX.

Contents

Table of cases

Preface

The Key Cases series is designed to give a clear understanding of important cases. This is useful when studying a new topic and invaluable as a revision aid.

Each case is broken down into fact and law. In addition, many cases are extended by the use of important extracts from the judgment or by comment or by highlighting problems. In some instances students are reminded that there is a link to other cases or material. If the link case is in another part of the same Key Cases book, the reference will be clearly shown. Some links will be to additional cases or materials that do not feature in the book.

To give a clear layout, symbols have been used at the start of each component of the case. The symbols are:

 Key Facts – These are the basic facts of the case.

 Key Law – This is the major principle of law in the case, the *ratio decidendi*.

 Key Judgment – This is an actual extract from a judgment made on the case.

 Key Comment – Comments made on the case.

 Key Problem – Apparent inconsistencies or difficulties in the law.

 Key Link – This indicates other cases which should be considered with this case.

The Key Link symbol alerts readers to links within the book and also to cases and other material especially statutory provisions which is not included.

At the start of each chapter there are mind maps highlighting the main cases and points of law. In addition, within most chapters, one or two of the most important cases are boxed to identify them and stress their importance.

Each Key Case book can be used in conjunction with the Key Facts book on the same subject. Equally they can be used as additional material to support any other textbook.

This Key Cases book covers the main areas of the English Legal System. However, the sections on judicial precedent and statutory interpretation are by far the biggest as these are very important topics in case law. This makes this book useful for those studying English Legal Method as well as those studying English Legal System.

The law is stated as I believe it to be on 1st February 2011.

Jacqueline Martin

1

Judicial Precedent

Binding Effect

Automatic Telephone and Electric Co Ltd v Registrar of Restrictive Trading Agreements Agreement (1965)
A judgment has immediately binding effect on lower courts and on appellate courts of the same standing

Kleinwort Benson Ltd v Lincoln City Council (1998)
An overruled case is regarded as never having been law

R v Gotts (1992)
Obiter dicta statements can create persuasive precedent

Court Hierarchy

Broome v Cassell & Co (1971)
Decisions by higher courts are binding on all lower courts

Miliangos v George Frank (Textiles) Ltd (1975)
The Court of Appeal must follow decisions of the House of Lords (now the Supreme Court)

Judicial Precedent (1)

The House of Lords (now the Supreme Court)

Practice Statement [Judicial Precedent] (1966)
The House of Lords was normally bound by their own past decisions but could depart from them where 'it appeared right to do so'

Conway v Rimmer (1968)
First use of Practice Statement

Herrington v British Railways Board (1972)
First use of Practice Statement in main-stream area of law

R v Shivpuri (1986)
First use of Practice Statement in criminal case

R v R and G (2003)
Use of Practice Statement to overrule major decision on the meaning of recklessness

1.1 The doctrine of precedent

 Schweppes Ltd v Registrar of Restrictive Trading Agreements [1965] 1 All ER 195 and Automatic Telephone and Electric Co Ltd v Registrar of Restrictive Trading Agreements Agreement [1965] 1 All ER 206

 Key Facts

Both cases involved the same point of law on discovery of documents in restrictive trade practices. In the *Schweppes* case Willmer LJ dissented with the majority decision. The *Automatic Telephone* case was heard by the same three judges later on the same day. In this case Willmer LJ accepted that he was now bound by precedent and agreed with the decision of the other two judges.

 Key Law

A judgment has immediate binding effect on an appellate court of the same standing (and also on any lower court).

 Key Judgment: Willmer LJ

'It seems to me, however, that I am now bound by the decision of the majority in the previous case. In these circumstances I have no alternative but to concur in saying that the appeal in the present case should be allowed.'

 Kleinwort Benson Ltd v Lincoln City Council [1998] 4 All ER 513

Key Facts

A financial arrangement known as 'interest rate swap transaction' was held to be unlawful by the Court of Appeal in 1991. Many local authorities had entered into such an arrangement prior to this date. A claim was made by the bank for the return of the money given to the council under the arrangement on the basis that the money had been paid under a mistake of law. An earlier Court of Appeal case had held that money paid under a mistake of law was not recoverable. The House of Lords ruled in *Kleinwort* that the bank could rely on the mistake of law, even though, at the time the agreement was made, it was legal under the law as it was thought to be at time.

Key Law

When a point of law is decided by overruling an earlier case, the overruled case is regarded as never having been the law and it is not applied in later cases or the instant case. This is so even though the agreement that is the subject of the claim was made before the earlier case was overruled.

Key Judgment: Lord Browne-Wilkinson

'The theoretical position has been that judges do not make or change law: they discover and declare the law which is throughout the same. According to this theory, when an earlier decision is overruled the law is not changed: its true nature is disclosed, having existed in that form all along. This theoretical position is, as Lord Reid said, a fairy tale in which no longer anyone believes. In truth, judges make and change the law. The whole of the common law is judge-made and only by judicial change in the law is the common law kept relevant in a changing world.'

Key Comment

Although the declaratory theory is no longer regarded as the position, precedent still has a retrospective effect. This can lead to the unjust situation that parties in the instant case will have relied on the law as it was at the time of the making of the agreement, only to be told that it is not the law and never has been.

(HL) R v Gotts [1992] 1 All ER 832

Key Facts

A 16 year-old-boy stabbed his mother after his father, who was known to be a violent man, threatened to kill him if he did not do this. The mother survived the stabbing and the son was charged with attempted murder. He claimed the defence of duress. In *R v Howe* (see above) the Law Lords stated, *obiter*, that duress should not be available to a defendant charged with attempted murder. The House of Lords in Gotts applied this principle, even though it was only an *obiter* statement.

Key Law

Obiter dicta statements in a judgment can create persuasive precedent.

1.2 The hierarchy of the courts

(HL) **Broome v Cassell & Co [1971] 2 All ER 187 CA,
[1972] 1 All ER 801 HL**

 Key Facts

The Court of Appeal held that the House of Lords' decision
in *Rookes v Barnard* (1964) on the circumstances in which
exemplary damages could be awarded was wrong. The
Court of Appeal pointed out that the House of Lords had
ignored earlier decisions in *Hulton & Co v Jones* (1910) and
Ley v Hamilton (1935). When *Broome v Cassell* was appealed to
the House of Lords, they held that the Court of Appeal was
bound to follow decisions of the House of Lords.

 Key Law

Decisions by higher courts are binding on all lower courts.

 Key Judgment: Lord Hailsham

'It is not open to the Court of Appeal to give advice to the judges
of first instance to ignore decisions of the House of Lords … The
fact is, and I hope it will never be necessary to say so again, that,
in the hierarchical system of courts which exists in this country, it
is necessary for each lower tier, including the Court of Appeal, to
accept loyally the decisions of the higher tiers.'

N.B. This now also applies to Supreme Court decisions.

(HL) **Miliangos v George Frank (Textiles) Ltd [1975]
1 All ER 1076 CA, [1975] 3 All ER 801 HL**

 Key Facts

The claimant (M), who was a Swiss national, supplied yarn to an
English company under a contract which provided for payment to
be made in Swiss francs. The company failed to pay and M made
a claim in the English courts. He asked that the award be in Swiss
francs and not in English pounds as the value of the pound had
fallen. There was a House of Lords decision, *Re United Railways of
Havana* (1960), which stated that judgments could only be given
in pounds and not in any other currency. The Court of Appeal in

Schorsch Meier GmbH v Hennin (1975) (see 1.4) had refused to follow this decision of the House of Lords. The House of Lords held that the change in the stability of the pound was a good reason to depart from their earlier decision, but they also pointed out that the Court of Appeal had no right to do this.

 Key Law

(1) The House of Lords had power under the Practice Statement to overrule its own past decisions.

(2) Lower courts are bound to follow decisions of higher courts.

Key Judgment: Lord Simon

'Courts which are bound by the rule of precedent are not free to disregard an otherwise binding precedent on the ground that the reason which led to the formulation of the rule embodied in such precedent seems to the court to have lost cogency.'

 Key Comment

It seems likely that if the Court of Appeal, in *Schorsch Meier GmbH v Hennin*, had not departed from the decision of the House of Lords in *Re United Railways of Havana*, then the case of *Miliangos* may never have been appealed to the House of Lords. This would have meant that the House of Lords did not have the opportunity to review its earlier decision.

1.3 The House of Lords

 Practice Statement [Judicial Precedent] [1966] 3 All ER 77

 Key Facts

'Their Lordships regard the use of precedent as an indispensable foundation upon which to decide what is the law and its application to individual cases. It provides at least some degree of certainty upon which individuals can rely in the conduct of their affairs, as well as a basis for orderly development of legal rules.

Their Lordships nevertheless recognise that the rigid adherence to precedent may lead to injustice in a particular case and also unduly restrict the proper development of the law. They, therefore, propose to modify their present practice and while treating former decisions of this House as normally binding, to depart from a previous decision when it appears right to do so.

In this connection they will bear in mind the danger of disturbing retrospectively the basis on which contracts, settlement of property and fiscal arrangements have been entered into and also the especial need for certainty as to the criminal law.

This announcement is not intended to affect the use of precedent elsewhere than in this House.'

N.B. Although this does not technically apply to the Supreme Court, that court is also prepared to overrule its own past decisions.

(HL) Conway v Rimmer [1968] 1 All ER 874

Key Facts

In an earlier case, *Duncan v Cammell, Laird and Co* (1947), the House of Lords had held that an affidavit sworn by a Government minister was sufficient to enable the Crown to claim privilege not to disclose the documents covered by that affidavit. The court was not even entitled to inspect the documents. In the present case, the House of Lords relied on the Practice Statement to depart from their earlier decision. They held that a minister's affidavit was not binding on the court and the court could always inspect the documents to decide whether 'public interest immunity' should be granted.

Key Law

The House of Lords had the right under the Practice Statement to depart from an earlier decision.

Key Comment

This was the first case in which the House of Lords used the Practice Statement to depart from an earlier decision.

(HL) Herrington v British Railways Board [1972] AC 877

Key Facts

A six-year-old boy was badly burned when playing on a railway track. The Railway Board knew that the fence alongside the railway line was damaged and that children had been seen playing on the track for some weeks before the boy was injured. A previous decision of the House of Lords in *Robert Addie & Sons (Collieries Ltd) v Dumbreck* (1929) had ruled that an occupier did not owe a duty of care to a trespasser. The House of Lords relied on the Practice Statement to overrule the *Robert Addie* case and to restate the law on the extent of duty of care owed by an occupier to a trespasser.

Key Law

The Practice Statement could be used to overrule old cases where social attitudes had changed.

(HL) R v Shivpuri [1986] 2 All ER 334

Key Facts

D thought he was dealing in prohibited drugs. In fact it was snuff and harmless vegetable matter. In an earlier case, *Anderton v Ryan* (1985), the House of Lords had held that there could not be an attempt in this sort of situation. However, in Shivpuri, they accepted that their decision in *Anderton v Ryan* had been wrong and used the Practice Statement to overrule it, even though that case had been decided only a year earlier.

Key Law

Even though the Practice Statement stressed need for 'especial certainty as to the criminal law', the House of Lords could use it to overrule an earlier case in the criminal law as well as in civil law.

Key Judgment: Lord Bridge

'I am undeterred by the consideration that the decision in *Anderton v Ryan* was so recent. The 1966 Practice Statement is an effective abandonment of our pretention to infallibility. If a serious error embodied in a decision of this House has distorted the law, the sooner it is corrected the better.'

R v G and R [2003] UKHL 50

 Key Facts

The defendants were two boys aged 11 and 12 years. They set fire to some bundles of newspapers which they threw under a large wheelie bin in a shop yard. The bin caught fire and this spread to the shop and other buildings causing about £1 million damage. The boys were convicted under both s 1 and s 3 of the Criminal Damage Act 1971 on the basis of objective recklessness (i.e. that an ordinary adult would have realised the risk). On appeal the House of Lords quashed their conviction and overruled the decision in *Metropolitan Police Commissioner v Caldwell* (1981), holding that the Law Lords in that case had 'adopted an interpretation of section 1 of the 1971 Act which was beyond the range of feasible meanings'.

 Key Law

The House of Lords was entitled to use the Practice Statement to overrule previous decisions.

Following House of Lords / Supreme Court

Miliangos v George Frank (Textiles) Ltd (1975)
The Court of Appeal must follow decisions of the House of Lords/Supreme Court

Mendoza v Ghaidan (2002)
The Court of Appeal may take into account European Court of Human Rights decisions in preference

Own past decisions

Young v Bristol Aeroplane Co Ltd (1944)
Court of Appeal is normally bound by its own past decisions

There are 3 exceptions:
- conflicting past decisions
- decision of House of Lords/Supreme Court which effectively overrules CA decision
- *per incuriam*

Davis v Johnson (1978)
The Court of Appeal must follow its own past decisions unless one of the exceptions in **Young's case** applies

Judicial Precedent (2)
Court of Appeal

Per incuriam

Williams v Fawcett (1985)
Refused to follow earlier decisions as they were based on error

Rickards v Rickards (1989)
Refused to follow earlier decision where the effect of a statute had been overlooked

The *per incuriam* power should only be used in 'rare and exceptional cases'

Criminal division

R v Taylor (1950)
May refuse to follow an earlier decision if the law was misapplied or misunderstood

R v Gould (1968)
Criminal Division of the Court of Appeal does not have to follow precedent as rigidly as the Civil Division

R v Spencer (1986)
Criminal Division is subject to the same rules as the Civil Division except that it may refuse to follow precedent where liberty is at stake

R v Simpson (2003)
Criminal Division has a residual discretion to refuse to follow a previous decision

1.4 The Court of Appeal

 Schorsch Meier GmbH v Hennin [1975] 1 All ER 152

Key Facts

The court had to consider whether damages had to be awarded in sterling or whether they could be in another currency. There was a decision by the House of Lords in the *Havana Railway* case (1960) that damages had to be in sterling. The Court of Appeal refused to follow this because sterling was no longer a stable currency. Justice required that damages be awarded in German marks otherwise the claimant would not have received the true value of his claim.

Key Law

See next case.

Miliangos v George Frank [Textiles] Ltd [1975] 1 All ER 1076, CA, [1975] 3 All ER 801 HL

Key Facts

See 1.2.

Key Law

The Court of Appeal is bound to follow decisions of the House of Lords and the Supreme Court.

➡ **Key Link**

Broome v Cassell & Co [1971] 2 All ER 187 CA, [1972] 1 All ER 801 HL (see 1.2).

Mendoza v Ghaidan [2002] EWCA Civ 1533

Key Facts

The Court of Appeal (Civil Division) 'revisited' the House of Lords' decision in *Fitzpatrick v Sterling Housing Association* (2001) on the application of the Rent Act 1977. They did this because s 2 of the Human Rights Act 1998 requires courts to 'take into account' decisions of the European Court of Human Rights.

Key Law

Where there is a human rights issue, the Court of Appeal (and all other courts) must take into account decisions of the European Court of Human Rights. This can lead to the Court of Appeal following a decision of the European Court of Human Rights in preference to a decision of the Supreme Court or the House of Lords.

 Key Link

The Court of Appeal also preferred a decision by the European Court of Human Rights to that of the House of Lords in *Director General of Fair Trading v The Proprietary Association of Great Britain* (2001).

CA **Young v Bristol Aeroplane Co Ltd [1944] 2 All ER 293**

 Key Facts

A workman, who had already received compensation under the Workman's Compensation Acts for injuries suffered at work, claimed damages from his employer. The defence argued that an earlier decision of the Court of Appeal prevented a claim for damages where statutory compensation had been received. It was held that the Court of Appeal had to follow its own past decisions.

Key Law

The Court of Appeal (Civil Division) is normally bound by its own previous decisions. However, *Young's case* set out three exceptions to this rule:

- where there are conflicting decisions in past Court of Appeal cases, the court can choose which one it will follow and which it will reject
- where there is a decision of the House of Lords which effectively overrules a Court of Appeal decision the Court of Appeal must follow the the decision of the House of Lords (now the Supreme Court)
- where the decision was made *per incuriam*, that is carelessly or by mistake because a relevant Act of Parliament or other regulation has not been considered by the court.

 Key Judgment: Lord Greene MR

'We have come to the clear conclusion that this court is bound to follow previous decisions of its own ... The only exceptions to this rule ... we here summarise: (1) The court is entitled and bound to decide which of two conflicting decisions of its own it will follow. (2) The court is bound to refuse to follow a decision of its own which, though not expressly overruled, cannot, in its opinion, stand with a decision of the House of Lords. (3) The court is not bound to follow a decision of its own if it is satisfied that the decision was given *per incuriam*.'

Davis v Johnson [1978] 1 All ER 1132

Key Facts

A young unmarried mother applied for an injunction ordering her violent partner to leave their flat. The tenancy of the flat was in their joint names. Earlier cases in the Court of Appeal had held that an injunction could not be granted where the partner had a right in the property (in this case a tenancy). The Court of Appeal refused to follow its earlier decisions. On appeal to the House of Lords, it was held that the earlier cases had been wrongly decided, but the House of Lords reminded the Court of Appeal that they were bound to follow its own previous decisions, subject to the exceptions in *Young's case*.

Key Law

The Court of Appeal is bound to follow its own previous decisions, subject to the exceptions in *Young's case*.

Key Judgment: Court of Appeal, Lord Denning

'While this court should regard itself as normally bound by a previous decision of the court, nevertheless it should be at liberty to depart from it if it is convinced that the previous decision was wrong. What is the argument to the contrary? It has been said that if an error has been made, this court has no option but to continue the error and leave it to be corrected by the House of Lords. The answer is this: the House of Lords may never have an opportunity to correct the error; and thus it may be perpetuated indefinitely, perhaps for ever.'

Key Judgment: House of Lords, Lord Diplock

'In an appellate court of last resort a balance must be struck between the need on the one hand for the legal certainty resulting from the binding effect of previous decisions and, on the other side, the avoidance of undue restriction on the proper development of the law. In the case of an intermediate appellate court, however, the second desideratum can be taken care of by appeal to a superior appellate court, if reasonable means of access to it are available; while the risk to the first desideratum, legal certainty, if the court is not bound by its own previous decisions grows ever greater. So the balance does not lie in the same place as a court of last resort.'

Key Comment

The judgments in this case demonstrate the arguments for and against the Court of Appeal having more freedom to depart from its own previous decisions. It is noticeable that since this case, the Court of Appeal has always followed the decisions of the House of Lords and the Supreme Court, except where there has been a decision of the European Court of Justice, the European Court of Human Rights (or in one exceptional case, the Privy Council – see *R v James*: *R v Karimi* (2006)).

 CA ## Williams v Fawcett [1985] 1 All ER 787

Key Facts

The issue was about the formalities necessary for a notice to commit someone for contempt. There had been four previous Court of Appeal decisions on the point. The court refused to follow these earlier decisions on the ground that they were based on error.

Key Law

The Court of Appeal is not bound to follow a previous decision of its own if that decision was reached per incuriam.

 CA ## Rickards v Rickards [1989] 3 All ER 193

Key Facts

An ex-husband failed to appeal within the time limits following a financial order in divorce proceedings. His later application for an extension of time to appeal was refused. He appealed to the Court of Appeal. There were previous decisions of the court holding that it had no authority to hear such an appeal. There was, however, a statutory provision to the contrary. The Court of Appeal, therefore, refused to follow its previous decisions and held that it could hear the appeal.

Key Law

The Court of Appeal can refuse to follow a previous decision of its own, if that decision was made in error where the effect of an earlier decision has been misunderstood. This power should only be used in 'rare and exceptional cases'.

Key Judgment: Lord Donaldson

'This court is justified in refusing to follow one of its own previous decisions not only where that decision is given in ignorance or forgetfulness of some statutory provision or some authority binding upon it, but also, in rare and exceptional cases, if it is satisfied that the decision involved a manifest slip or error.'

Key Comment

This case was considered to be 'rare and exceptional' because:

(a) a wrongful denial of jurisdiction was a serious matter amounting to breach of a statutory duty on the part of the Court of Appeal; and

(b) it was most unlikely (because of the cost involved) that the House of Lords would be presented with an opportunity to correct the mistake.

 Key Link

Rakhit v Carty [1990] 2 All ER 202.

1.5 The Court of Appeal (Criminal Division)

 (CAA) R v Taylor [1950] 2 KB 368

Key Facts

D had been convicted of bigamy. The issue was whether a defence of absence of the spouse for seven years was available only for a second marriage (a view held in a previous case) or whether it was also available for any subsequent marriage. The Court of Criminal Appeal (the court which existed prior to the creation of the Court of Appeal (Criminal Division)) refused to follow the previous case and held that the defence was available.

Key Law

Where the issue involved the liberty of the subject, a court of appeal may refuse to follow its own previous decision if the law has been misapplied or misunderstood.

Key Judgment: Lord Goddard CJ

'This court, however, has to deal with questions involving the liberty of the subject, and it finds on reconsideration, that, in the opinion of a full court assembled for that purpose, the law has either been misapplied or misunderstood in a decision which it has previously given, and that, on the strength of that decision, an accused person has been sentenced to imprisonment, it is the bounden duty of the court to reconsider the earlier decision with a view to seeing whether that person had been properly convicted. The exceptions which apply in civil cases ought not to be the only ones applied in such a case as the present.'

(CA) R v Gould [1968] 1 All ER 849

Key Facts

D was convicted of bigamy. The issue was whether an honest and reasonable belief that, at the date of the second marriage, the first marriage had been dissolved, was a good defence. The earlier case of *R v Wheat*: *R v Stocks* (1921) had ruled that such a mistake was not a good defence. The court held that it was not bound to follow its own previous decision and quashed the conviction.

Key Law

In cases which involve the liberty of the subject, the Criminal Division of the Court of Appeal does not have to apply the doctrine of precedent as rigidly as the Civil Division.

Key Judgment: Diplock LJ

'In its criminal jurisdiction which it has inherited from the Court of Criminal Appeal, the Court of Appeal does not apply the doctrine of *stare decisis* with the same rigidity as in its civil jurisdiction. If on due consideration we were to be of the opinion that the law had been either misapplied or misunderstood in an earlier decision of this court, or its predecessor the Court of Criminal Appeal, we should be entitled to depart from the view as to the law expressed in the earlier decision notwithstanding that the case could not be brought within any of the exceptions laid down in *Young v Bristol Aeroplane Co Ltd*.'

R v Spencer [1985] 1 All ER 673 CA, [1986] 2 All ER 928 HL

Key Facts

The issue before the court was whether the Court of Appeal (Criminal Division) was bound by a previous decision of its own.

Key Law

The Criminal Division of the Court of Appeal is subject to the same rules of precedent as the Civil Division, save that when the liberty of the subject is at stake, it may decline to follow one of its own previous decisions.

R v Simpson [2003] EWCA 1499

Key Facts

Following D's plea of guilty to charges involving fraudulent evasion of VAT, the judge at the Crown Court made a confiscation order in the sum of £209,351. D appealed against this on the basis that a notice had not been served as required under s 72 of the Criminal Justice Act 1988. In a case in 2002 the Court of Appeal (Criminal Division) had held that defects in such a notice meant that the Crown Court did not have jurisdiction to make a confiscation order. The court refused to follow the earlier decision.

Key Law

The Court of Appeal (Criminal Division), in a five judge court, decided that it had a residual discretion to decide whether one of its previous decisions should be treated as a binding precedent when there were grounds for saying that that decision was wrong.

The Privy Council

Tai Hing Ltd v Liu Chong Hing Bank (1986)
The Privy Council is normally bound to follow House of Lords/Supreme Court decisions

Doughty v Turner Manufacturing Co Ltd (1964)
Privy Council decisions are not binding on courts in the English legal system but they are highly persuasive

R v James: R v Karimi (2006)
Where there are conflicting decisions of the House of Lords or Supreme Court and Privy Council, English courts should normally follow the decision of the House of Lords or Supreme Court. In the exceptional circumstances of this case the decision of the Privy Council would be followed

Divisional Court

Huddersfield Police Authority v Watson (1947)
The Divisional Court is bound by its own past decisions subject to the same exceptions in Young's case

R v Greater Manchester Coroner, ex p Tal (1984)
In criminal cases and judicial review the Divisional Court can depart from a previous decision if that decision was wrong

High Court

Colchester Estates (Cardiff) v Carlton Industries (1984)
The later of two conflicting decisions in the High Court should be followed

Judicial Precedent (3)

Distinguishing

Merritt v Merritt (1970)
The parties had agreed to separate, so the case could be distinguished from **Balfour v Balfour (1919)**

Boardman v Sanderson (1964)
The fact that D knew parent was in vicinity distinguished this case from **King v Phillips (1953)**

Judicial law-making

Donoghue v Stevenson (1932)
The tort of negligence was developed by judicial decision

R v R (1991)
Judges ruled that marital rape was a criminal offence

C v DPP (1995)
Judges refused to change the law on the presumption that children under 14 were doli incapax

R v Clegg (1995)
Judicial law-making is permissible but should be exercised with caution

1.6 Precedent and other courts

(PC) Tai Hing Ltd v Liu Chong Hing Bank [1986] 1 AC 80

Key Facts

This was an appeal from Hong Kong to the Judicial Committee of the Privy Council. The issue was whether the Privy Council was bound to follow a decision of the House of Lords. They held that they were.

Key Law

Where the development of law in the country from which the appeal originates is the same as that in England and Wales, the Judicial Committee of the Privy Council is bound to follow decisions of the House of Lords.

Key Judgment: Lord Scarman

'Once it is accepted … that the applicable law is English, their Lordships of the Judicial Committee will follow a House of Lords' decision which covers the point in issue. The Judicial Committee is not the final judicial authority for the determination of English law. That is the responsibility of the House of Lords.'

(CA) **Doughty v Turner Manufacturing Co Ltd [1964] 1 QB 518**

Key Facts

The issue was on remoteness of damage in negligence. The Court of Appeal followed a decision by the Judicial Committee of the Privy Council in *Overseas Tankship (UK) Ltd v Morts Dock & Engineering Co Ltd (The Wagon Mound)* (1961) in preference to a previous decision of its own, *Re Polemis* (1921).

Key Law

Decisions by the Judicial Committee of the Privy Council are not binding on courts in the English legal system, but they are highly persuasive.

(CA) **R v James: R v Karimi [2006] EWCA Crim 14**

 Key Facts

In both cases D was charged with murder. At both trials the judge had directed the jury that the law on provocation was stated by the Judicial Committee of the Privy Council in *A-G for Jersey v Holley* (2005) rather than as stated by the House of Lords in *Smith (Morgan)* (2001). D appealed on the ground that the House of Lords decision was the one that governed English law. The Court of Appeal held that in the exceptional circumstances of *A-G for Jersey v Holley* the decision of the Privy Council was to be preferred.

 Key Law

Where there is conflict between decisions of the House of Lords or Supreme Court and the Judicial Committee of the Privy Council, the normal rule is that courts in the English legal system are bound by the House of Lords' or Supreme Court's decision. However, in exceptional circumstances, courts may follow the Privy Council.

 Key Comment

The case of *Holley* was exceptional in that nine of the twelve Law Lords formed the panel for the case and the decision was reached on a majority of six to three. The judges stated in their judgments that the result reached by the majority clarified definitively the English law.

(DC) **Huddersfield Police Authority v Watson [1947] 2 All ER 193**

 Key Facts

The Divisional Court had to decide whether it was bound by its own previous decision in *Garvin v Police Authority for City of London* (1944). It held it was bound by its own previous decisions.

 Key Law

The Divisional Court is bound by its own previous decisions, subject to the same exceptions as in *Young v Bristol Aeroplane Co Ltd* (1944) (see 1.4).

R v Greater Manchester Coroner, ex p Tal [1984] 3 All ER 240 (DC)

Key Facts

The Queen's Bench Divisional court refused to follow its own previous decision in *R v Surrey Coroner, ex p Campbell* (1982) and held that it did have supervisory power over coroners' courts.

Key Law

In criminal cases and in judicial review cases the Divisional Court can depart from its own previous decisions if it is convinced that the previous decision was wrong.

➡ Key Link

R v Stafford Justices, ex p Customs and Excise Commissioners [1991] 2 All ER 201.

DPP v Butterworth [1994] 1 AC 381.

Colchester Estates (Cardiff) v Carlton Industries [1984] 2 All ER 601 (HC)

Key Facts

The claimant wanted to bring an action against his tenant for cost of maintenance repairs to the tenanted property. There had been two earlier decisions on this point. In 1981 a judge in the High Court had ruled that permission from the court was required for such an action to be brought. In 1984 another High Court judge ruled that permission was not required. It was held that the later decision should be followed, so permission was not required.

Key Law

Generally, the later of two conflicting decisions in the High Court should be followed in subsequent cases in the High Court.

Key Comment

Where the first case has not been cited to the judge in the second case, then the second decision can be considered *per incuriam* and the judge in the third case may choose which decision he prefers. This was not the position in *Colchester Estates* as the 1981 case had been cited to the judge in the 1984 case.

1.7 Distinguishing

(CA) **Balfour v Balfour [1919] 2 KB 571**

Key Facts

A husband had to go abroad to work but his wife was unable to go with him because of illness. The husband agreed that he would pay his wife an allowance of £30 per month. He failed to pay the allowance and the wife sued him for breach of contract. The action failed as there was no intention to create legal relations. There was merely a domestic arrangement.

Compare this to the next case.

(CA) **Merritt v Merritt [1970] 1 WLR 1121**

Key Facts

A husband had deserted his wife for another woman. He and his wife came to an agreement that the husband would pay her £40 per month: the wife would pay the mortgage on their house and, when the mortgage was paid off, the husband would transfer his share of the house to her. This part of the agreement was written down. The husband later refused to transfer the house. The wife claimed for breach of contract. The court held there was an enforceable contract and that the husband was in breach of contract.

Key Law

The court distinguished the second case from the first case on the facts. In *Balfour*, although the parties were living apart, they were not separated. Their arrangement was purely a domestic matter. In *Merritt*, the parties had separated and, following this, they had made an agreement part of which was in writing. Although they were still husband and wife, their agreement was clearly meant as a legally enforceable contract.

(CA) **King v Phillips [1953] 1 QB 429**

Key Facts

A mother suffered nervous shock when, from 70 yards away, she saw a taxi reverse into her small child's cycle. She thought the child had been injured, though in fact he had not. Her claim in negligence failed because she was too far away from the incident and outside the range of foresight of the defendant.

Compare this to the next case.

 CA Boardman v Sanderson [1964] 1 WLR 1317

 Key Facts

D negligently reversed his car over the claimant's son's foot just outside C's house. D knew that C was within earshot and likely to run to the scene. C was able to recover damages for nervous shock.

 Key Law

This case was distinguished from *King v Phillips* on the basis that D knew the parent was in close vicinity of the incident and therefore likely to be affected by it.

1.8 Judicial law making

 HL Donoghue v Stevenson [1932] AC 562

Key Facts

The appellant drank some ginger beer which was contaminated by a snail being in the bottle. This made her ill. She had not bought the drink so she had no remedy in contract. So she sued the drinks manufacturer. The House of Lords ruled that a manufacturer owed a duty of care to the ultimate consumer.

Key Law

The tort of negligence developed from the decision in this case.

Key Comment

This case shows how judicial decisions can create vast areas of law. The main development of the law on negligence came from *obiter dicta* where Lord Atkin put forward the 'neighbour' test for establishing whether a duty of care is owed.

 HL R v R (Rape: Marital Exemption) [1991] 4 All ER 481

 Key Facts

D and his wife had separated and agreed to seek a divorce. Three weeks later D broke into the wife's parents' home, where she was staying, and attempted to rape her.

Key Law

Although old authorities stated that a man could not be guilty of raping his wife, the law had to evolve to suit modern society. D could be guilty.

Key Judgment: Lord Keith of Kinkel

'[The] question is whether ... this is an area where the court should step aside to leave the matter to the parliamentary process. This is not the creation of a new offence, it is the removal of a common law fiction which has become anachronistic and offensive and we consider that it is our duty, having reached that conclusion, to act upon it.'

Key Comment

D took the case to the European Court of Human Rights claiming that the retrospective recognition of marital rape was a breach of Art 7 of the European Convention on Human Rights. Marital rape was not a crime at the time D committed the act, but he was still found guilty of the offence. It was held that there was no breach of Art 7. In fact, abandoning the idea that a husband could not be prosecuted for rape of his wife, conformed to one of the fundamental objectives of the Convention, that of respect for human dignity.

(HL) C v DPP [1995] 2 All ER 43

Key Facts

A 12-year-old boy was charged with interfering with a motor vehicle with intent to commit theft. The defence relied on the common law presumption of *doli incapax* which meant that a child aged between 10 and 14 could not be convicted unless the prosecution proved that he knew that his act was seriously wrong. He was convicted. On appeal to the Divisional court it was held that the *doli incapax* presumption was outdated and no longer good law. The case was then appealed to the House of Lords who allowed the appeal. They held that the presumption was still part of English law and that the courts did not have the right to abolish it.

Key Law

Where the issue is not a purely legal one, then law making should be left to Parliament.

Key Judgment: Lord Lowry

'Whatever change is made, it should come only after collating and considering the evidence and after taking account of the effect which a change would have on the whole law relating to children's antisocial behaviour. This is a classic case for Parliamentary investigation, deliberation and legislation.'

Key Comment

Parliament did legislate to change the law in the Crime and Disorder Act 1998. This abolished the presumption of *doli incapax*.

(HL) R v Clegg [1995] 1 All ER 334

Key Facts

D was a soldier on duty at a checkpoint in Northern Ireland. A car failed to stop at the checkpoint and D was shouted at to stop it. D fired four shots at the car. One of the shots killed a passenger in the car. The evidence was that the car was some 50 yards past the checkpoint by the time the fatal shot was fired. D was convicted of murder. The House of Lords refused to allow a defence of self-defence to succeed where the force used was excessive in the circumstances.

Key Law

Judicial law-making is permissible but should be exercised with discretion. Major changes in the law are for Parliament to make.

Key Judgment: Lord Lowry

'I am not averse to judges developing law, or indeed making new law, when they can see their way clearly, even when questions of social policy are involved ... But in the present case I am in no doubt that your Lordships should abstain from law-making. The reduction of what would otherwise be murder to manslaughter in a particular class of case seems to me essentially a matter for decision by the legislature, and not by the House in its judicial capacity.'

2

Legislation

Parliamentary Acts

R (Jackson and others) v Attorney General (2005)
Parliament has power to amend the 1911 Parliament Act to the extent of the amendment contained in the 1949 Act

Parliamentary sovereignty

British Railways Board v Pickin (1974)
No court is entitled to go behind an Act once it has been passed

Burmah Oil Co Ltd v Lord Advocate (1965)
Parliament can pass retrospective legislation

R v Secretary for State for Transport, ex p Factortame (1990)
EU law is supreme over national law

Legislation

Delegated legislation

R v Secretary of State for the Home Office, ex p Fire Brigades Union (1995)
Delegated legislation could not replace an existing statutory scheme

Aylesbury Mushrooms Ltd (1972)
Where the correct procedure is not carried out, delegated legislation can be *ultra vires*

R (Haw) v Secretary of State for Home Department (2005)
Delegated legislation cannot amend or extend primary legislation

Strickland v Hayes (1896)
Delegated legislation can be declared void if it is unreasonable

2.1 The Parliament Acts 1911 and 1949

 R (Jackson and others) v Attorney General [2005] UKHL 56

 Key Facts

There was a challenge to the legality of the Hunting Act 2004 which had been passed under the Parliament Acts. It was argued that Parliament could not use the 1911 Parliament Act to pass the 1949 Parliament Act and that any legislation passed by virtue of s 2 of the 1911 Act was only delegated legislation. The House of Lords held that Parliament had power to amend the 1911 Parliament Act to the extent of the amendment contained in the 1949 Act.

 Key Law

The 1911 Act made the fundamental change of allowing the consent of the House of Lords to be dispensed with. The 1949 Act left the relationship between the House of Lords and the House of Commons substantially the same as it was before the 1949 Act. The 1949 Act only reduced the length of the period for which the House of Lords could delay legislation.

2.2 Parliamentary sovereignty

 British Railways Board v Pickin [1974] 1 All ER 609

Key Facts

A private Act of Parliament, the British Railways Act 1968, was enacted by Parliament. It was challenged on the basis that that the British Railways Board had fraudulently concealed certain matters from Parliament. This had led to Parliament passing the Act which had the effect of depriving *Pickin* of his land or proprietary rights. The action was struck out as frivolous.

 Key Law

No court is entitled to go behind an Act once it has been passed. No challenge can be made to an Act of Parliament even if there was fraud.

Burmah Oil Co Ltd v Lord Advocate [1965] AC 75

 Key Facts

During WW2, British forces destroyed oil installations belonging to Burmah Oil in order to prevent them falling into the hands of the invading Japanese forces. The company sued the Crown for compensation. The House of Lords held that compensation was payable. The government then passed the War Damage Act 1965 avoiding the payment of compensation in such situations. This Act was given retrospective effect so that no damages had to be paid to Burmah Oil.

 Key Law

Parliament has the power to pass legislation that has retrospective effect. Such legislation takes precedence over any court decision.

R v Secretary for State for Transport, ex p Factortame (Case C-213/89) [1990] ECR 1-2433

 Key Facts

The UK Parliament passed the Merchant Shipping Act 1988. This Act provided that, for a fishing vessel to be registered in the UK, the majority of the ownership had to be held by UK nationals. This provision was in conflict with provisions under EU law and the Act of Parliament was held to be invalid as against EU nationals.

 Key Law

Where an Act of Parliament is in conflict with EU legislation, then the EU legislation takes priority. There is supremacy of EU law over national law.

2.3 Delegated legislation

R v Secretary of State for the Home Office, ex p Fire Brigades Union [1995] 2 All ER 244

Key Facts

The Home Secretary set up a Criminal Injuries Compensation Scheme by prerogative order. There was a statutory scheme (under the Criminal Justice Act 1988) already in existence.

Key Law

Delegated legislation could not replace an existing statutory scheme. The Home Secretary's scheme was void.

Agricultural, Horticultural and Forestry Industrial Training Board v Aylesbury Mushrooms Ltd [1972] 1 All ER 280

(QBD)

Key Facts

Before establishing an agricultural training board, legislation obliged the Minister of Labour to consult 'any organisation appearing to him to be representative of substantial numbers of employers engaging in the activity concerned'. He failed to consult the Mushroom Growers' Association which represented about 85 per cent of all mushroom growers. As a result the order establishing a training board was invalid as against mushroom growers.

Key Law

Where the correct procedure is not carried out, delegated legislation can be *ultra vires* and invalid.

R v Secretary of State for Education and Employment, ex p National Union of Teachers [2000] All ER (D) 991

(DC)

Key Facts

The Education Act 1996 gave the Secretary of State for Education and Employment power to set conditions for appraisal of teachers and access to higher rates of pay. The Secretary allowed only four days for consultation. In addition the scheme went beyond the powers laid down in the Act. The scheme was held to be void, on both substantive and procedural grounds.

(1) Where insufficient time is allowed for consultation, the delegated legislation is procedurally *ultra vires*.
(2) Where delegated legislation goes beyond the powers given in the enabling Act, it is substantively *ultra vires*.

R (Haw) v Secretary of State for the Home Department [2005] EWHC 2061 (Admin)

Key Facts

Since June 2001 Mr Haw had been carrying on a demonstration in Parliament Square against the Government's policies on Iraq. In 2005 Parliament passed the Serious Organised Crime and Police Act 2005. Section 132 of this Act made it a requirement that those demonstrating in and around Parliament Square should get authorisation before starting the demonstration. The section was brought into effect by a statutory instrument which made it an offence to continue a demonstration without authorisation. Mr Haw successfully challenged the validity of this. It was held to be void as it created a new criminal offence which was not contained in the Act.

Key Law

Delegated legislation cannot amend or extend primary legislation, especially where it would create a new criminal offence. Any delegated legislation which purports to do this is *ultra vires*.

Key Comment

[2006] EWCA Civ 532

The case was appealed to the Court of Appeal where it was decided as a point of interpretation that s 132 applied to demonstrations starting both before and after the commencement of the Act. This meant that there was nothing in the case which contradicted the Act. The Court of Appeal did not therefore consider the point of whether delegated legislation can or cannot amend or extend primary legislation.

 ## Strickland v Hayes [1896] 1 QB 290

Key Facts

A byelaw prohibiting the singing or reciting of any obscene song or ballad, and the use of obscene language generally, was held to be unreasonable as it was not limited to public places nor did it require the prohibited acts to be done to the annoyance of the public.

Key Law

Delegated legislation can be declared void if it is unreasonable.

 Percy v Hall [1996] 4 All ER 523

Key Facts

Several people were arrested for offences of entering a protected military area in breach of byelaws. The court had to decide if the byelaws were sufficiently certain or whether they were void for uncertainty. It was held in the circumstances they were not sufficiently certain.

(1) Delegated legislation which is unclear or uncertain can be declared void.
(2) If the wording is merely ambiguous then, wherever possible, any reasonable meaning should be given to the byelaw.

Key Judgment

Simon Brown LJ supported the test put forward by Lord Denning in *Fawcett Properties Ltd v Buckingham County Council* (1960) when he said:

'I can well understand that a byelaw will be held void for uncertainty if it can be given no meaning or no sensible or ascertainable meaning. But if the uncertainty stems only from the fact that the words of the byelaw are ambiguous, it is well settled that it must, if possible, be given such a meaning as to make it reasonable and valid, rather than unreasonable and invalid.'

3

Statutory Interpretation

The Literal Rule

R v Judge of the City of London Court (1892)
The literal meaning of words should always be taken, even if the result is absurd

Fisher v Bell (1960)
Whiteley v Chappell (1868)
Both illustrate an absurd result by using the literal rule

London & North Eastern Railway Co v Berriman (1946)
An example of an unfair decision through use of the literal rule

Magor and St Mellons RDC v Newport Corp (1950)
Literal rule used but judges disagreed on its use

Statutory Interpretation (1) The Three 'Rules'

The Golden Rule

Grey v Pearson (1857)
Literal meaning to be used unless it leads to absurdity or repugnance

R v Allen (1872)
Golden rule used to avoid absurdity of no-one being guilty of bigamy

Adler v George (1964)
Words modified to avoid an absurd result

Re Sigsworth (1935)
Literal meaning NOT taken as it would have been repugnant

The Mischief Rule

Heydon's case (1584)
The courts should consider the gap the Act was passed to prevent

Smith v Hughes (1960)
Mischief rule used rather than literal meaning of the words

Royal College of Nursing v DHSS (1981)
Application of the mischief rule to prevent the 'mischief' of back-street abortions

DPP v Bull (1994)
Reports can be looked at to discover the mischief

3.1 The Literal Rule

(CA) **R v Judge of the City of London Court [1892] 1 QB 273**

Key Facts

The court had to decide whether the City of London Court had jurisdiction to hear the case under the County Courts Admiralty Jurisdiction Acts. If so this would give the court power to award up to £300 in damages. If not, then the maximum damages would be £50.

Key Law

The words of the Acts were given their literal meaning.

Key Judgment: Lopez LJ

'I have always understood that, if the words of an Act are unambiguous and clear, you must obey those words, however absurd the result may appear; and, to my mind, the reason for this is obvious. If any other rule were followed, the result would be that the court would be legislating instead of the properly constituted authority of the country, namely, the legislature.'

(DC) **Fisher v Bell [1960] 1 QB 394**

Key Facts

D was a shop-keeper, who had displayed a flick knife marked with a price in his shop window; but had not actually sold any. He was charged under s 1(1) of the Restriction of Offensive Weapons Act 1959. The section made any person who sells or hires or offers for sale or hire a flick-knife guilty of an offence. The court had to decide whether he was guilty of offering the knife for sale. There is a technical legal meaning in contract law of 'offer'. This has the effect that displaying an article in a shop window is not an offer; it is only an invitation to treat. The Court of Appeal held that under the literal legal meaning of 'offer', the shop-keeper had not made an offer to sell and so was not guilty of the offence.

Key Law

A literal interpretation was used.

Key Comment

In this case the outcome was clearly not what Parliament intended as they amended the law by the Registration of Offensive Weapons Act 1961 to cover the display of knives in shop windows.

Whiteley v Chappell (1868) 4 LR QB 147

Key Facts

D was charged under a section which made it an offence to impersonate 'any person entitled to vote'. D had pretended to be a person whose name was on the voters' list, but who had died. The court held that D was not guilty since a dead person is not, in the literal meaning of the words, 'entitled to vote'.

Key Law

A literal interpretation was used, even though it meant D was acquitted.

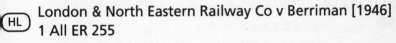

(HL) London & North Eastern Railway Co v Berriman [1946] 1 All ER 255

Key Facts

Mr Berriman was a railway worker who was hit and killed by a train while doing maintenance work, oiling points on a railway line. A regulation made under the Fatal Accidents Act stated that a look-out should be provided for men working on or near the railway line 'for the purposes of relaying or repairing' it. Mr Berriman was not relaying or repairing the line; he was maintaining it. His widow claimed compensation for his death because the railway company had not provided a look-out man while Mr Berriman had to work on the line. It was held that the relevant regulation did not cover maintenance work, so Mrs Berriman's claim failed.

Key Law

A literal interpretation was used, even though the regulations were intended to improve safety for those working on railway lines.

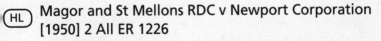

(HL) Magor and St Mellons RDC v Newport Corporation [1950] 2 All ER 1226

Key Facts

The Newport Extension Act 1934 extended the county borough of Newport to include the areas of Magor and St Mellons. The Act provided that these two Rural District Councils should receive reasonable compensation. Immediately after the Act took effect the two Rural District Councils were amalgamated to form a new District Council. The court had to decide whether this new Council had a right to compensation. It was held that it had no right.

Key Law

A literal interpretation of the law was used.

Key Comment

This case is important for the conflict between Lord Denning in his dissenting judgment in the Court of Appeal and the judgment of the House of Lords, as shown in these quotes:

Key Judgment: Lord Denning

'We sit here to find out the intention of Parliament and carry it out, and we do this better by filling in the gaps and making sense of the enactment than by opening it up to destructive analysis.'

Key Judgment: Lord Scarman

'If Parliament says one thing but means another, it is not, under the historic principles of the common law, for the courts to correct it. The general principle must surely be acceptable in our society. We are to be governed not by Parliament's intentions but by Parliament's enactments.'

3.2 The Golden Rule

(HL) **Grey v Pearson (1857) 6 HL Cas 61**

The facts and decision are not important in the context of statutory interpretation. The significant point of the case is the definition of the golden rule in Lord Wensleydale's judgment.

Key Judgment: Lord Wensleydale

'[T]he grammatical and ordinary sense of the words is to be adhered to, unless that would lead to some absurdity or some repugnance or inconsistency with the rest of the instrument, in which case the grammatical and ordinary sense of the words may be modified, so as to avoid that absurdity and inconsistency, but no further.'

(CCR) **R v Allen (1872) LR 1 CCR 367**

Key Facts

D was charged under s 57 of the Offences Against the Person Act 1861 which made it an offence to 'marry' whilst one's original spouse was still alive (and there had been no divorce). The question for the court was the exact meaning of marry. Did it mean become legally married (in which case D was not guilty as he could not legally marry whilst the first marriage existed) or go through a ceremony of marriage? The court held that it meant go through a ceremony of marriage. D was therefore guilty of bigamy.

Key Law

The golden rule was used to avoid the absurdity of the section being ineffective. If the literal meaning of 'legally marry' had been used, then no-one could ever have been guilty of bigamy.

(DC) Adler v George [1964] 1 All ER 628

Key Facts

D was prosecuted under the Official Secrets Act 1920 for an offence of obstructing HM forces 'in the vicinity of' a prohibited place. D had obstructed HM forces but was inside the prohibited place. The Divisional Court read the Act as being 'in or in the vicinity of' and held that D was guilty.

Key Law

The golden rule was used to modify the words of the Official Secrets Act 1920, in order to avoid the absurdity of being able to convict someone who was near (in the vicinity of) a prohibited place but not being able to convict someone who carried out the obstruction in the place.

(HC) Re Sigsworth [1935] Ch 89

Key Facts

A son had murdered his mother. The mother had not made a will, so normally her estate would have been inherited by her next of kin, according to the rules set out in the Administration of Justice Act 1925. This meant that the murderer-son would have inherited as her 'issue'. There was no ambiguity in the words of the Act, but the court held that the literal meaning of the word should not apply. The son could not inherit.

Key Law

The golden rule can be used to prevent a repugnant situation. Here it was the repugnancy of the son inheriting.

Key Comment

The court was, in effect, writing into the Act that the 'issue' would not be entitled to inherit where they had killed the deceased.

This result of the case would also be achieved by applying the purposive approach (see 3.5).

3.3 The Mischief Rule

Heydon's Case (1584) Co Rep 7a

The facts and decision are not important in the context of statutory interpretation. The significant point of the case is the definition of the mischief rule.

 Key Law

In interpretation of a statute, there are four points the court should consider. In the original language of the case these are:

'1st What was the Common Law before the making of the Act.

2nd What was the mischief and defect for which the Common Law did not provide.

3rd What remedy the Parliament hath resolved and appointed to cure the disease of the commonwealth.

And, 4th The true reason of the remedy; and then the office of all Judges is always to make such construction as shall suppress the mischief, and advance the remedy.'

(DC) **Smith v Hughes [1960] 2 All ER 859**

 Key Facts

Six women had been convicted under s 1(1) of the Street Offences Act 1959 which stated that 'It shall be an offence for a common prostitute to loiter or solicit in a street or public place for the purpose of prostitution'. In each case they argued on appeal that they were not 'in a street or public place' as required by the Act for them to be guilty. One woman had been on a balcony and the others had been at the windows of ground floor rooms, with the window either half open or closed. In each case the women were attracting the attention of men by calling to them or tapping on the window. The court decided that they were guilty.

 Key Law

The court should look at the mischief which the Act was designed to prevent.

Key Judgment: Lord Parker CJ

'For my part I approach the matter by considering what is the mischief aimed at by this Act. Everybody knows that this was an Act to clean up the streets, to enable people to walk along the streets without being molested or solicited by common prostitutes. Viewed in this way it can matter little whether the prostitute is soliciting while in the street or is standing in the doorway or on a balcony, or at a window, or whether the window is shut or open or half open.'

 Key Link

Eastbourne Council v Stirling [2000] EWHC Admin 410.

HL Royal College of Nursing v DHSS [1981] 1 All ER 545

 ### Key Facts

Under s 1(1) of the Abortion Act 1967, abortion is legal 'when a pregnancy is terminated by a registered medical practitioner' in specific circumstances. When the Act was passed in 1967 the procedure to carry out an abortion was by surgery so that only a doctor (a registered medical practitioner) could do it. In 1973 a new medical technique allowed pregnancy to be terminated by inducing premature labour with drugs. The first part of the procedure for this was carried out by a doctor, but the second part could be performed by nurses without a doctor present. The Department of Health and Social Security issued a circular giving advice that it was legal for nurses to carry out the second part of the procedure. The Royal College of Nursing sought a declaration that the circular was wrong in law. It was held to be lawful.

 ### Key Law

The application of the mischief rule was preferred to the literal rule.

 ### Key Judgment: Lord Diplock

'The Abortion Act 1967 which it falls to this House to construe is described in its long title as "An Act to amend and clarify the law relating to termination of pregnancy by registered medical practitioners". Whatever may be the technical imperfections of its draftsmanship, however, its purpose in my view becomes clear if one starts by considering what was the state of the law relating to abortion before the passing of the Act, what was the mischief that required amendment, and in what respect was the existing law unclear.'

Key Comment

The decision that the procedure was lawful under the Abortion Act 1967 was made by a three to two majority. The dissenting judges were very opposed to the decision. Lord Edmund Davies stated that to read the words 'terminated by a registered medical practitioner' as meaning 'terminated by treatment for the termination of pregnancy in accordance with recognised medical practice' was redrafting the Act 'with a vengeance'.

(DC) DPP v Bull [1994] 4 All ER 411

Key Facts

Bull was a male prostitute charged with an offence against s 1(1) of the Street Offences Act 1959. The case was dismissed by the magistrate on the ground that the words 'common prostitute' only applied to female prostitutes. The prosecution appealed by way of case stated. The Divisional Court considered the Wolfenden Report, Cmnd 247, 1957, which had led to the passing of the Act. That report clearly identified the mischief as being one created by women. The court held that the words were only meant to apply to women. They did not cover male prostitutes.

Key Law

A report may be considered in order to discover the mischief an Act was intended to remedy.

Extrinsic aids

Black Clawson case (1975)
To identify the mischief, reports leading to the passing of an Act may be considered

R v R and G (2003)
Law Commission report considered in overruling an earlier case

Fothergill v Monarch Airines (1980)
Travaux préparatoires can be consulted where the law implements an International Convention

Pepper v Hart (1993)
Hansard may be consulted if the legislation is ambiguous or obscure or leads to an absurdity

Wilson v First County Trust (2003)
Consulting Hansard is not contrary to the Bill of Rights

Laroche v Spirit of Adventure (2009)
A wide range of extrinsic aids used

Statutory Interpretation (2) The Purposive Approach and Aids to Interpretation

The rules of language

Powell v Kempton Park Race Course (1899)
Where there is a list followed by a general term, the general term is limited to items of the same kind as the list

Allen v Emmerson (1944)
There must be at least two specific types in the list for this rule to apply

Tempest v Kilner (1846)
A list not followed by general words is limited to the items in the list

Inland Revenue v Frere (1965)
Words must be considered in context

The purposive approach

Jones v Tower Boot Co Ltd (1997)
Interpretation should promote the purpose of Parliament

R (Quintavalle) v Secretary of State (2003)
The law should give effect to Parliament's purpose where there was a later scientific development

3.4 The rules of language

(HL) **Powell v Kempton Park Race Course [1899] AC 143**

Key Facts

D was charged with keeping a 'house, office, room or other place for betting'. He had been operating betting at what is known as Tattersall's ring, which is outdoors. The House of Lords decided that the general words 'other place' had to refer to indoor places since all the words in the list were indoor places and so the defendant was not guilty.

Key Law

Where there are specific words followed by a general term, the general term is limited to the same kind of items as the specific words.

(DC) **Allen v Emmerson [1944] All ER 344**

Key Facts

The court had to interpret the phrase 'theatres and other places of amusement' and decide if it applied to a funfair. As there was only one specific word 'theatres', it was decided that a funfair did come under the general term 'other places of amusement' even though it was not of the same kind as theatres.

Key Law

There must be at least two specific categories for the *ejusdem generis* rule to operate.

Tempest v Kilner (1846) 3 CB 249

Key Facts

The court had to consider whether the Statute of Frauds 1677, which required a contract for the sale of 'goods, wares and merchandise' of more than £10 to be evidenced in writing, applied to a contract for the sale of stocks and shares. The list 'goods, wares and merchandise' was not followed by any general words, so the court held that only contracts for those three types of things were affected by the statute; because stocks and shares were not mentioned they were not caught by the statute.

Key Law

Where there is a list of words which is not followed by general words, then the legislation applies only to the items in the list.

 Inland Revenue Commissioners v Frere [1965] AC 402

Key Facts

The section of the relevant Income Tax Act set out rules for 'interest, annuities or other annual interest'. The first use of the word 'interest' on its own could have meant any interest paid, whether daily, monthly or annually. Because of the words 'other annual interest' in the section, the court decided that 'interest' only meant annual interest.

Key Law

Words must be looked at in context and interpreted accordingly. This may involve looking at other words in the same section or at other sections in the Act.

3.5 The purposive approach

 Jones v Tower Boot Co Ltd [1997] 3 All ER 406

Key Facts

The complainant suffered verbal and physical abuse from two fellow employees because of his racial background. He claimed his employers were liable for this conduct under s 32(1) of the Race Relations Act 1976 which provides that:

> 'Anything done by a person in the course of his employment shall be treated for the purposes of the Act … as done by his employer as well as by him, whether or not it was done with the employer's knowledge or approval.'

The employers argued that they were not liable as racial abuse was not within the course of employment. This was supported by the principles of vicarious liability in the law of tort. The court pointed out that the purpose of the Act was to eradicate racial discrimination and held that the employers were liable.

Key Law

The interpretation should be such as to promote the purpose of Parliament.

Key Comment

The decision in this case can be contrasted with that in *Fisher v Bell* (see 3.1) where a special legal meaning of the words in the law of contract was taken, even though this was clearly not what Parliament had intended in the criminal law. Here the special legal meaning of the words was rejected in favour of the purpose of Parliament.

 (HL) **R (Quintavalle) v Secretary of State [2003] UKHL 13**

Key Facts

The issue was whether organisms created by cell nuclear replacement (CNR) came within the definition of 'embryo' in the Human Embryology and Fertilisation Act 1990. Section 1(1)(a) states that 'embryo means a live human embryo where fertilisation is complete'. CNR was not possible in 1990 and the problem is that fertilisation is not used in CNR. It was held that CNR did come within the definition of 'embryo'.

Key Law

The courts should give effect to Parliament's purpose.

Key Judgment: Lord Bingham

'[T]he court's task, within permissible bounds of interpretation is to give effect to Parliament's purpose … Parliament could not have intended to distinguish between embryos produced by, or without, fertilisation since it was unaware of the latter possibility.'

3.6 Extrinsic aids

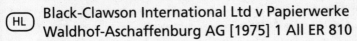

(HL) Black-Clawson International Ltd v Papierwerke
Waldhof-Aschaffenburg AG [1975] 1 All ER 810

Key Facts
There was a dispute over the enforcement of a foreign judgment
which involved the interpretation of s 8(1) of the Foreign
Judgments (Reciprocal Enforcement) Act 1933. The court had
to decide whether it could look at a report which had led to the
passing of the Act. It held that it could do so in order to discover
the mischief which the Act had been passed to remedy.

Key Law
Where there is an ambiguity in a statute, the court may have regard
to a report which resulted in the passing of the Act in order to
ascertain the mischief the Act was intended to remedy.

➡ Key Link
DPP v Bull [1994] 4 All ER 411.

(HL) R v R and G [2003] UKHL 50

Key Facts
Two young boys set fire to some newspapers in a shop yard. After
they left the fire spread to the shop itself and to other shops. They
were charged with arson under the Criminal Damage Act 1971. The
court had to decide the meaning of 'reckless' in the Act. Prior to the
passing of the Act there had been a report by the Law Commission.
However, in *Metropolitan Police Commissioner v Caldwell* (1981),
the House of Lords had refused to look at the report but instead
gave an objective meaning to recklessness (i.e. that a defendant
would be guilty if an ordinary adult would have realised the
risk). The court consulted the report and overruled Caldwell
holding that the report showed that subjective recklessness
was required.

Key Law
Reports leading to the passing of legislation can be considered by
the courts.

Key Judgment: Lord Bingham

'[S]ection 1 as enacted followed, subject to an immaterial addition, the draft proposed by the Law Commission. It cannot be supposed that by "reckless" Parliament meant anything different from the Law Commission. The Law Commission's meaning was made plain both in its Report (Law Com No 29, 1970) and in Working Paper No 23 which preceded it. These materials (not, it would seem, placed before the House in *R v Caldwell*) reveal a very plain intention to replace the old expression "maliciously" by the more familiar expression "reckless" but to give the latter expression the meaning which *R v Cunningham* [1957] 2 QB 396 had given to the former ... No relevant change in the *mens rea* necessary for the proof of the offence was intended, and in holding otherwise the majority misconstrued section 1 of the Act.'

(HL)

Fothergill v Monarch Airlines Ltd [1980] 2 All ER 696

Key Facts

The case involved interpretation of the Carriage by Air Act 1961 and the Warsaw Convention 1929 which was contained in a schedule to the Act. The court held it could look at *travaux préparatoires* (explanatory notes published with the Convention) in order to understand its true effect.

Key Law

The original Convention should be considered along with any preparatory materials or explanatory notes published with an International Convention as it was possible that, in translating and adapting the Convention to our legislative process, the true meaning of the original might have been lost.

(HL) **Pepper (Inspector of Taxes) v Hart [1993] 1 All ER 42**

Key Facts

Teachers were charged reduced fees for their children at an independent school. This concession was a taxable benefit. The question was exactly how the calculation of the amount to be taxed should be done. Under the Finance Act this had to be done on the 'cash equivalent' of the benefit. Section 63 of the Finance Act 1976 defined 'cash equivalent' as 'an amount equal to the cost of the benefit, and further defined the 'cost of the benefit' as 'the amount of any expense incurred in or in connection with its provision'. This was ambiguous as it could mean either:

(a) the marginal (or additional) cost to the employer of providing it to the employee (this on the facts was nil) (the decision); or

(b) the average cost of providing it to both the employee and the public (this would involve the teachers having to pay a considerable amount of tax).

Key Law

Hansard could be consulted on the intention of Parliament when passing an Act of Parliament.

Key Judgment: Lord Browne-Wilkinson

'The exclusionary rule should be relaxed so as to permit reference to parliamentary materials where; (a) legislation is ambiguous or obscure, or leads to an absurdity; (b) the material relied on consists of one or more statements by a minister or other promoter of the Bill together if necessary with such other parliamentary material as is necessary to understand such statements and their effect; (c) the statements relied on are clear. Further than this I would not at present go.'

(HL) Wilson v First County Trust Ltd (No 2) [2003] UKHL 40

Key Facts

The Speaker of the House of Commons and the Clerk of the Parliament were joined in the case to make representations against the use of Hansard for the purpose of deciding compatibility of an Act with the European Convention on Human Rights. The court held that *Hansard* could be consulted, though in the actual case *Hansard* did not provide any assistance with interpretation.

Key Law

Consulting *Hansard* did not amount to a 'questioning' of what is said in Parliament and so was not contrary to s 1 of Art 9 of the Bill of Rights 1688.

Key Judgment: Lord Nicholls

'The courts would be failing in the due discharge of the new role assigned to them by Parliament if they were to exclude from consideration relevant background information whose only source was a ministerial statement in Parliament or an explanatory note prepared by his department while the Bill was proceeding through Parliament.

By having such material the court would not be questioning proceedings in Parliament or intruding improperly into the legislative process or ascribing to Parliament the views expressed by a minister. The court would merely be placing itself in a better position to understand the legislation.'

Key Comment

It is noticeable that the judgment extends beyond *Hansard* as it clearly states, *obiter*, that the court also has a duty to consider explanatory notes.

(CA) Laroche v Spirit of Adventure [2009] EWCA Civ 12

Key Facts

C suffered injuries due to the sudden landing of a hot air balloon in which he had taken a flight. He started his action for damages against Ds nearly three years later. It was held that the balloon was an 'aircraft', there had been 'carriage' of C and that C was a 'passenger'. These findings meant that Sch 1 of the Carriage by Air Acts (Application of Provisions) Order 1967 applied and the claim had to be brought within two years of the incident. C was out of time in starting his case and it was dismissed for this reason.

Key Law

In interpreting the 1967 Order, the court considered the following external aids:

- the Warsaw Convention which applies to international flights: even though this was not an international flight, it was held that the 1967 Order should be interpreted in a similar way
- the Pocket Oxford English Dictionary which defined 'aircraft' as 'aeroplane(s), airship(s) and balloon(s)'
- another statutory instrument, the Air Navigation Order 2000.

4

European Union Law

Effect of EU sources of law

Van Duyn v Home Office (1974)
Treaties can confer rights on which individuals can rely

Macarthys v Smith (1979)
An individual can enforce a right in EU law

Commission v UK: Re Tachograph (1979)
EU regulations are binding in their entirety on Member States

Marshall v Southampton and South West Hampshire Area Health Authority (1986)
Directives have vertical direct effect and can be relied on by individuals against the State

Duke v GEC Reliance Ltd (1988)
Directives do not have horizontal direct effect and cannot be relied on against a private organisation or individual

Grimaldi v Fond des Maladies Professionelles (1989)
Recommendations do not have binding effect but must be taken into account by national courts

European Union Law

Supremacy of EU law

Van Gend en Loos v Nederlandse Administratie (1963)
EU law takes precedence over national law

R v Secretary of State for Transport, ex p Factortame (1990)
EU law is supreme over national law even when the national law has been passed subsequent to the relevant EU law

4.1 Sources of EU law

 (ECJ) Van Duyn v Home Office [1975] 3 All ER 190

 Key Facts

The UK refused to allow a member of the Church of Scientology to enter the country. This contravened the freedom of movement of workers under what was then Art 39 of the Treaty of Rome, but the UK relied on the right to derogate on the grounds of public policy as contained in Directive 64/221. It was held that the Treaty conferred individual rights which could be relied on, but, in the circumstance of this case, the UK could derogate from those rights.

 Key Law

Individuals can rely in English law on rights given by the Treaties setting out European Union Law.

(ECJ) **Macarthys v Smith [1979] WLR 1189**

 Key Facts

A woman discovered that she was being paid less than her less-qualified male predecessor in the job. She was the only one doing that work in the company and therefore could not rely on English law as there was no male comparator. She claimed discrimination under what was then Art 141 of the Treaty of Rome (as worded prior to the reworking of the Treaty under the Treaty of Amsterdam). It was held that the she could rely directly on the Treaty.

Key Law

Primary legislation (treaties) of the European Union which conferred rights on individuals was of direct effect and could be relied on, even when national law was contrary to EU law.

(ECJ) **Commission v UK: Re Tachographs [1979] ECR 419**

Key Law

Council Regulation EEC/1463/70 made it compulsory for tachographs (mechanical recording equipment) to be fitted to certain types of vehicle. The UK brought the regulation into effect through a Statutory Instrument which provided for a voluntary system of fitting tachographs. It was held that the fitting was compulsory.

EU Regulations are directly binding in their entirety. They cannot be applied by Member States in an incomplete or selective manner.

Marshall v Southampton and South West Hampshire Area Health Authority [1986] 2 All ER 584

Key Facts

The applicant, a woman, had been forced to retire before the age of 65, while men were allowed to work until that age. A reference was made to the European Court of Justice on the point of whether this amounted to discrimination under the Equal Access Directive 76/207. The court held that the rights conferred by the Directive could be relied on as against the State.

Key Law

Directives have vertical direct effect.

(HL) Duke v GEC Reliance Ltd [1988] 1 All ER 626

Key Facts

The facts were the same as in *Marshall* (above). However, the employer was a private body and not the state. It was held that the Directive did not give rights against private bodies.

Key Law

Directives do NOT have horizontal direct effect.

(ECJ) Grimaldi v Fond des Maladies Professionelles [1989] ECR 4407

Key Facts

A Belgian tribunal made a reference to the European Court of Justice as to the standing of a Commission recommendation. It was held that national courts, when deciding a case, must take relevant recommendations into account.

Key Law

Recommendations do not have binding effect but must be taken into account.

4.2. Supremacy of EU law

 Van Gend en Loos v Nederlandse Administratie [1963] ECR 1

 Key Facts

It was held that a re-classification of import duties by the Dutch Government contravened the then Art 12 of the Treaty of Rome.

 Key Law

EU law takes precedence over national law.

 R v Secretary for State for Transport, ex p Factortame [1990] ECR 1-2433, [1991] 1 All ER 70

 Key Facts

The Merchant Shipping Act 1988 was passed by Parliament to protect British fishing. It required that the majority ownership of a company had to be in the hands of UK nationals for a ship to be registered to fish in British waters. It was held that this contravened the 'non-discrimination on nationality' rule in the then Art 12 of the Treaty of Rome.

 Key Law

EU law is supreme over national law.

 Key Judgment: Judge Rapporteur, CN Kakouris

'[A]ny provision of a national legal system and any legislation, administrative, or judicial practice which might impair the effectiveness of Community law … are incompatible with those requirements which are the very essence of EC law.'

5

The Legal Profession

Solicitors' duty of care

Ross v Caunters (1979)
Solicitors can be liable to third parties where their negligence causes a foreseeable loss

White v Jones (1995)
A solicitor owes a duty of care to a third party (e.g. a beneficiary)

The Legal Profession

Advocates' immunity

Hall, Arthur J S, & Co v Simons (2000)
Advocates are no longer immune from claims in negligence

5.1 Solicitors' duty of care

(HC) Ross v Caunters [1979] 3 WLR 605

Key Facts

Solicitors prepared a will for a client and sent it to him for it to be signed and witnessed. They failed to warn him that the will should not be witnessed by the spouse of any beneficiary. One of the witnesses was the husband of a beneficiary. As a result she was not able to inherit under the will. She sued the solicitors for the loss suffered. The solicitors claimed that they only had a duty of care to the testator. The judge held that they owed a duty of care to the beneficiary.

Key Law

Solicitors can be liable to a third party, where their negligence causes that third party a foreseeable loss.

Key Judgment: Megarry V-C

'If one examines the facts of the case before me to discover whether the three-fold elements of the tort of negligence exist, a simple answer would be on the following lines. First, the solicitors owed a duty of care to the plaintiff since she was someone within their direct contemplation as a person so closely and directly affected by their acts and omissions in carrying out their client's instructions to provide her with a share of his residue that they could reasonably foresee that she would be likely to be injured by those acts and omissions. Second, there has undoubtedly been a breach of that duty of care; and third, the plaintiff has clearly suffered loss as a direct result of that breach of duty.'

Key Comment

It had previously been accepted that solicitors owed a duty of care to their client, but this case extended the scope of a solicitors' duty of care. This principle was approved by the House of Lords in *White v Jones* (1995) (see below).

(HL) **White v Jones [1995] 1 All ER 691**

Key Facts

A solicitor was instructed by a client to change the client's will so that his daughters (to whom he had previously left nothing) would receive £9,000 each. The solicitor delayed and did not do anything for some months, so that the client died without the change being made. The old will was effective and the daughters did not receive anything under it. They were successful in claiming £9,000 each from the solicitor.

Key Law

A solicitor owes a duty of care to an intended beneficiary of a will when instructed by the testator to draw up the will.

5.2 Advocates' immunity

(HL) **Hall, Arthur J S & Co v Simons [2000] 3 All ER 673**

Key Facts

Three cases were joined on appeal. In all three cases there was a claim against a firm of solicitors for negligence and, in each, the firm relied on the rule, established in *Rondel v Worsley* (1969) that an advocate was immune from any claim in negligence. The House of Lords held that it was no longer in the public interest that advocates should be immune from claims.

Key Law

The decision in *Rondel v Worsley* was overruled. Advocates are no longer immune from claims in negligence.

Key Comment

The House of Lords considered the four points given in *Rondel v Worsley* as reasons for immunity. These were:

1 Advocate's divided loyalty: an advocate owes a duty to the court as well as to his client. The Law Lords stated that removing immunity was unlikely to have a significantly adverse effect on any duty owed to the court.

2 Cab rank principle: this is a rule that barristers are obliged to accept any case, provided it is in the area of law in which they practise. It had been argued that a barrister who had to accept any client would be unfairly exposed to vexatious claims. The Law Lords stated that such a claim did not have any real substance.

3 The witness analogy: it is well established that a witness is absolutely immune from liability for anything he says in court. However, a witness does not owe anyone a duty of care. He only has a duty to tell the truth. A advocate has a duty of care to his client.

4 Protraction of litigation: allowing a claim for negligent advocacy could, in effect, lead to a re-trial of the original case. The Law Lords accepted that there might be a risk of this happening, but pointed out that, in criminal cases, starting a civil action for negligence while there was still an appeal route open to the defendant would normally be an abuse of process. Once a conviction had been set aside, then there could be no public policy objection to a claim for negligence. In civil cases, the outcome was only of interest to the parties and so there was no public interest objection to a subsequent finding that, but for the negligence of his advocate, the losing party would have won.

6

The Judiciary

Independence of the judiciary

R v Bow Street Magistrates, ex p Pinochet Ugarte (No 2) (1999)
A judge should disclose his position or stand down if he has a close connection to any party or connected organisation

Locabail (UK) Ltd v Bayfield Properties (2000)
A litigant has a fundamental right to a fair trial by an impartial tribunal

Director General of Fair Trading v The Proprietary Association of Great Britain (2001)
The test for bias of the tribunal is whether a fair-minded observer would conclude that there was a real possibility of bias

Lawal v Northern Spirit Ltd (2003)
An advocate who has previously sat as a judge with a panel of lay members must not appear in front of those same lay members in another case

---

6.1 Independence of the judiciary

 R v Bow Street Magistrates, ex p Pinochet Ugarte (No 2) [1999] 1 All ER 577

 Key Facts

An extradition warrant was issued from Spain for General Pinochet, the former President of Chile. It alleged his complicity in crimes of murder, torture and conspiracy to murder which occurred in Chile while he was President.

The English courts had to decide whether General Pinochet could rely on immunity as head of state at the time of the alleged crimes.

The House of Lords, on a three to two majority, rejected his right to claim immunity. Lord Hoffman was one of the majority but did not give reasons for his decision. Following the ruling, it was realised that Lord Hoffman was an unpaid director of the charitable trust run by Amnesty International. This was important because Amnesty had been granted leave to intervene in the proceedings and had made submissions to the Lords supporting the extradition.

The Law Lords set aside the decision on the basis that Lord Hoffman's involvement with Amnesty had invalidated the hearing.

 Key Law

A judge should disclose his position or stand down if he has a close connection and an active role with a charity or other organisation involved in the litigation.

 Locabail (UK) Ltd v Bayfield Properties [2000] 1 All ER 65

 Key Facts

Five cases were heard where there was an objection to the judge on the grounds of potential bias. Only in one of the five cases, *Locabail (UK) Ltd v Bayfield Properties*, was leave to appeal given. This was a personal injury case in which the judge hearing the matter had frequently expressed pro-claimant and anti-insurance company views in articles published in legal journals. The Court of Appeal held that it could not exclude the possibility that the judge might have unconsciously leant in favour of the claimant. The appeal was allowed and a retrial ordered.

 Key Law

(1) A litigant has a fundamental right to a fair trial by an impartial tribunal.

(2) The test set out by the House of Lords in *R v Gough* (1993) should be applied. The test is whether there is a real danger or possibility of bias.

 Director General of Fair Trading v The Proprietary Association of Great Britain [2001] 1 WLR 700

 Key Facts

A case was being heard before the Restrictive Practices Court with lay members on the panel. Part way through the case one lay member disclosed that, since the start of the case, she had applied for a job with one of the main witnesses for one of the parties to the case. The respondents argued that such behaviour must imply bias on her part and that the whole panel should stand down. The Court of Appeal upheld this argument.

Key Law

The test set out by the House of Lords in *R v Gough* (1993) should be refined in the light of the implementation of the Human Rights Act 1998. The test should now be whether a fair-minded observer would conclude that there was a real possibility of bias.

Key Comment

The test is in line with decisions by the European Court of Human Rights. The test in *R v Gough* was a subjective one on the part of the court. The new test is an objective one where the matter is considered from the perspective of a fair-minded observer.

(HL) Lawal v Northern Spirit Ltd [2003] UKHL 35

Key Facts

A QC appeared in front of the Employment Appeal Tribunal acting for D who was the employer of the claimant. The QC had previously sat as a part-time judge in the Employment Appeal Tribunal and one of the lay members in the present case had been on the panel with the QC. The claim was dismissed but on appeal to the House of Lords, they held that the practice of advocates, who were part-time judges, subsequently appearing in front of lay members of the tribunal with whom they had sat should be discontinued as it tended to undermine public confidence.

Key Law

The principle to be applied was whether a fair minded and informed observer would conclude that there was a real possibility of bias.

7

Juries

Jury qualifications

R v Richardson (2004)
The fact that a juror was disqualified because of a criminal conviction did not make a verdict unsafe

R v Abdoikov (2005)
An eligible juror should not be excluded merely because of their knowledge of the criminal justice system

Juries in civil cases

Ward v James (1966)
A jury should not normally be used in personal injury cases

H v Ministry of Defence (1991)
Exceptional circumstances are not sufficient in personal injury cases to justify trial by jury

Racz v Home Office (1994)
A close relationship to one of the torts where jury trial is normally ordered is not a factor to be taken into consideration

Goldsmith v Pressdram Ltd (1987)
Even where reputation is at stake, jury trial can be refused if the documentation is complex

Juries

Juries in criminal cases

R v Twomey and others (2009)
Order made for trial by a judge alone after jury tampering

KS v R (2010)
Order made for trial by a judge alone refused

R v Sheffield Crown Court, ex p Brownlow (1980)
Jury vetting is a breach of privacy and unconstitutional

R v Mason (1980)
Checking potential jurors for disqualifying convictions is permissible

R v Ford (1989)
If a jury has been randomly selected it cannot be challenged if it contains no ethnic minority jurors

Bushell's case (1670)
The jury is the sole arbiter of fact and must not be pressurised by the judge

R v McKenna (1960)
The jury must not be put under undue pressure when coming to a verdict

R v Pigg (1983)
It is sufficient if the foreman announces the number of jurors who agreed with the verdict on a finding by a majority verdict

7.1 Jury qualifications

 (CA) R v Richardson [2004] EWCA Crim 2997

 Key Facts

A person with a criminal conviction which disqualified them from sitting as a juror, sat as a juror. D appealed against his conviction on the basis that the presence of a disqualified person on the jury made the verdict unsafe.

 Key Law

The fact that a juror was disqualified because of a criminal conviction did not make a verdict unsafe.

 Key Judgment

The court cited with approval the judgment of Garland J in *R v Bliss* (1986) where he said that the Court of Appeal 'will not interfere with the verdict of a jury unless there is either evidence pointing directly to the fact or evidence from which a proper inference may be drawn that the defendant may have been prejudiced or may not have received a fair trial.'

 (CA) R v Abdoikov [2005] EWCA Crim 1986

 Key Facts

Three cases were heard together on appeal. In two of the cases a police officer had been on the jury; in the third case a CPS lawyer was on the jury. The defendants appealed on the basis that this made the trials appear unfair. The appeals were dismissed.

Key Law

Where a person was eligible to sit as a juror, they should not be excluded merely because of their knowledge of the criminal justice system.

 Key Judgment: Lord Woolf CJ

'A fair-minded and informed observer would not conclude that there was a real possibility that a juror was biased merely because his occupation was one which meant that he was involved in some capacity or other in the administration of justice.'

Key Comment
Prior to April 2004, people who were involved in the administration of justice (or who had been within the previous 10 years) were ineligible to sit as jurors. This ineligibility was removed by the Criminal Justice Act 2003.

7.2 Juries in civil cases

(CA) **Ward v James [1966] 1 All ER 563**

Key Facts
The claimant (C) was a passenger in a car which was involved in an accident. C was paralysed as a result and started an action in negligence against the car driver. C applied for trial by jury: this was ordered, but the Court of Appeal made *obiter* statements that the use of juries in personal injury cases should not be encouraged.

Key Law
A jury should not normally be used in a personal injury trial.

Key Judgment: Lord Denning MR
'Recent cases show the desirability of three things. First, assessability: in cases of grave injury, where the body is wrecked or the brain destroyed, it is very difficult to assess a fair compensation in money, so difficult that the award must basically be a conventional figure, derived from experience or from awards in comparable cases. Secondly, uniformity: there should be some measure of *uniformity* in awards so that similar decisions are given in similar cases; otherwise there will be great dissatisfaction in the community, and much criticism of the administration of justice. Thirdly, *predictability*: parties should be able to predict with some measure of accuracy the sum which is likely to be awarded in a particular case … None of these three is achieved when the damages are left at large to the jury.'

CA Hodges v Harland & Wolff [1965] 1 All ER 1086

Key Facts

The claimant was operating an air compressor in the course of his work. The spindle on the machine was not properly guarded and it caught the claimant's trousers and tore away his penis and scrotum. He was left with the urge for sexual activity but was unable to perform the sexual act. He applied for the case to be tried with a jury and the Court of Appeal granted this.

Key Law

Trial by jury in personal injury cases should only be allowed in exceptional cases.

Key Comment

In this case the Court of Appeal stated that the comments made in *Ward v James* did not mean that personal injuries cases could never be tried by a jury. However, this case appears to have been the last personal injury case to have been tried by jury.

CA H v Ministry of Defence [1991] 2 All ER 834

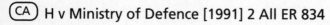

Key Facts

A soldier received negligent medical treatment which led to the need for a major part of his penis to be amputated. He applied for trial by jury but this was refused.

Key Law

The policy should be that as stated in *Ward v James*, i.e. that trial by jury is inappropriate for any personal injury action so far as the jury is required to assess compensating damages.

HL Racz v Home Office [1994] 2 WLR 23

Key Facts

The claimant alleged he had been held in prison on remand without justification. He made a claim for damages for misfeasance in public office in respect of the period for which he had been detained. He sought jury trial for this claim. Trial by jury was refused despite the fact that the action was closely related to false imprisonment. The fact that the claimant sought exemplary damages was also insufficient to justify trial by jury.

Key Law

Section 69(3) of the Supreme Court Act 1981 raises a presumption against jury trial. The fact that a claim has a close relationship to one of the torts for which s 69(1) retained the right to jury trial was not a factor to be taken into account in deciding whether it is appropriate to rebut the presumption.

Key Comment

This decision illustrates the reluctant of the courts to order trial by jury in civil actions.

CA Goldsmith v Pressdram Ltd [1987] 3 All ER 485

Key Facts

The claimant (C) was a director of a number of large international companies. The defendants (Ds) published an article in the satirical magazine, Private Eye, alleging that the claimant had been involved in secret share dealings. C started a defamation action against Ds. Ds applied for the case to be tried by a judge alone on the basis that their defence would involve detailed examination of complex multiple transactions carried out by the claimant. The judge made this order and the Court of Appeal upheld it.

Key Law

In deciding whether a case should be tried by jury, the fact that the alleged defamation concerned criminal conduct was not enough to outweigh the problems of lengthy examination of documents.

Key Judgment: Lawton LJ

'It is true that the allegation against [the claimant] is an unpleasant one. It charges him with criminal offences. His reputation, honour and integrity are, to some extent, in issue, but ... the fact that honour and integrity are under attack in a case is not an overriding factor in favour of trial with a jury ... This case, although it may be of importance to [the claimant], cannot be said to be one affecting national interest or national personalities. It is a long way from such a case and, having regard to its undoubted complexity and the difficulties which a jury will have in following the detail of evidence, in my judgment the discretion of the court should not be exercised in favour of the [claimant].'

7.3 Juries in criminal cases

 (CA) R v Twomey and others [2009] EWCA Crim 1035

 Key Facts

Ds were charged in connection with offences connected to a major robbery from a warehouse at Heathrow airport. Three previous trials had collapsed and there had been a serious attempt at jury tampering in the last of these. The prosecution applied, under the provisions of s 44 of the Criminal Justice Act 2003, for trial by a judge alone. The Court of Appeal ordered that the trial should be by judge alone.

 Key Law

Trial should be by judge alone as there was a very significant risk of jury tampering. Protective measures could not sufficiently address the extent of the risk. Also the proposed protective measures would have imposed a real burden on individual jurors.

(CA) KS v R [2010] EWCA Crim 1756

 Key Facts

An associate of D had tried to tamper with the jury during D's trial at Northampton Crown Court. As a result, the jury had to be discharged. The prosecution applied for the re-trial to take place without a jury under s 44 of the Criminal Justice Act 2003. A single judge granted this, but the Court of Appeal overturned the decision.

Key Law

The attempt to tamper with the jury had been opportunistic. It arose because of the 'casual arrangements' at the court for smokers, which enabled members of the public to mix with jurors. There was no evidence of careful planning. A fairly limited level of jury protection could reasonably be provided and this would outweigh the potential threat of future jury tampering in the case.

(CA) R v Sheffield Crown Court, ex p Brownlow [1980] 2 All ER 444

 Key Facts

Two police officers were due to be tried at the Crown Court on charges of assault. The defence solicitors sought an order that the prospective jury members be checked for criminal convictions. The judge made an order that the Chief Constable carry out such a check. The Chief Constable applied to the Divisional Court for the judge's order to be quashed. This was refused on the procedural point that the Divisional Court had no jurisdiction to review decisions made by a Crown Court judge. This point went to the Court of Appeal who confirmed that the Divisional Court had no jurisdiction. In the course of their judgments *obiter* comments were made on jury vetting.

Key Law

Obiter statement that jury vetting is a breach of privacy and is unconstitutional.

Key Judgment: Lord Denning MR

'To my mind it is unconstitutional for the police authorities to engage in "jury vetting". So long as a person is eligible of jury service and is not disqualified, I cannot think it right that, behind his back, the police should go through his record … If this sort of thing is to be allowed, what comes of a man's right to privacy?'

 CA R v Mason [1980] 3 All ER 777

Key Facts

D was tried for burglary and handling stolen property. Before the trial began, the police had checked the names of those summoned for jury service and given details of convictions to the prosecution. These convictions did not disqualify any juror from serving, but the prosecution used the information to ask for a panel member to stand by for the Crown (i.e. not be used as a juror unless there were insufficient others to form a panel). D argued on appeal that this was in breach of guidelines on jury vetting issued by the Attorney-General.

Key Law

Some scrutiny of the jury panel is necessary to ensure that disqualified persons are prevented from sitting on a jury. If such checks reveal other non-disqualifying convictions, then it is lawful for these to be given to the prosecution.

R v Ford [1989] 3 All ER 445

 Key Facts

The defendant, who was charged with driving without consent and reckless driving, was from an ethnic minority. The jury panel was entirely white. D applied for a multi-racial jury. The application was refused.

 Key Law

Random selection is the basis of jury selection. A jury that has been correctly randomly selected cannot be changed just because it does not contain any ethnic minority members.

 Key Judgment: Lord Lane LCJ

'The conclusion is that, however well intentioned the judge's motive might be, the judge has no power to influence the composition of the jury, and that it is wrong for him to attempt to do so. If it should ever become desirable that the principle of random selection should be altered, that will have to be done by way of statute and cannot be done by any judicial decision.'

Bushell's Case (1670) Vaugh 135

 Key Facts

Several jurors refused to convict Quaker activists of unlawful assembly. The trial judge would not accept the not guilty verdict, and ordered the jurors to resume their deliberations without food or drink. When the jurors persisted in their refusal to convict, they were fined and committed to prison until the fines were paid. On appeal, the Court of Common Pleas ordered the release of the jurors, holding that jurors could not be punished for their verdict.

 Key Law

A judge cannot pressurise a jury to return the verdict which he thinks is appropriate. The jury is the sole arbiter of fact in a criminal trial.

R v McKenna [1960] 1 QB 411

 ### Key Facts

The judge at the trial threatened the jury, who had been deliberating for about 2 hours and 15 minutes, that if they did not return a verdict within another 10 minutes they would be locked up all night. The jury then returned a verdict of guilty within six minutes. The defendant's conviction was quashed on appeal because of the judge putting undue pressure on the jury.

 ### Key Law

The jury, when coming to their verdict, must not be subject to undue pressure by the judge.

 ### Key Judgment: Cassels J

'It is a cardinal principle of our criminal law that in considering their verdict, concerning as it does, the liberty of the subject, a jury shall deliberate in complete freedom, uninfluenced by any promise, unintimidated by any threat. They still stand between the Crown and the subject, and they are still one of the main defences of personal liberty. To say to such a tribunal in the course of its deliberations that it must reach a conclusion within ten minutes or else undergo hours of personal inconvenience and discomfort, is a disservice to the cause of justice.'

R v Pigg [1983] 1 All ER 56

 ### Key Facts

When the foreman of the jury returned the jury's decision, he stated that it was a majority verdict and that 10 of the jury had agreed with the verdict. He did not state how many jurors had disagreed.

 ### Key Law

Provided the foreman announced the number who had agreed with the verdict and that number was within the number allowed for a majority verdict, then the conviction was legal. It did not matter that the foreman had not also been asked how many disagreed with the verdict.

Secrecy of jury room

R v Thompson (1962)
Evidence of what occurred in the jury room is not admissible

R v Young (1995)
The court can inquire into happenings outside of the jury room

Sander v UK (2000)
The judge should discharge the jury if there is an obvious risk of racial bias

R v Connor: R v Mirza (2004)
The rule that the court cannot hear evidence of events in the jury room is compatible with Art 6 of the European Convention on Human Rights

R v Karakaya (2005)
Jurors must decide the case on the evidence given in court. They cannot take into account outside information

Juries

Contempt of court

A-G v Associated Newspapers (1994)
Disclosure by publication is an offence even though the information was obtained from a indirect source

A-G v Scotcher (2005)
Any disclosure (other than to the court) of discussions in the jury room is contempt, even if D has a genuine belief that there has been a miscarriage of justice

7.4 Secrecy of the jury room

 R v Thompson [1962] 1 All ER 65

Key Facts

After the jury had announced a verdict of guilty but before the judge had passed sentence, one of the jurors told a member of the public that the jury had been in favour of acquitting D until the foreman had produced a list of the defendant's previous convictions. D appealed against his conviction but the Court of Criminal Appeal refused to accept evidence of what happened in the jury room and upheld the conviction.

Key Law

It is important to preserve the secrecy of the jury room. Evidence of what occurred in jury discussions cannot be given in evidence to support an appeal.

 R v Young [1995] QB 324

Key Facts

The defendant was charged with the murder of two people. The jury had to stay overnight in a hotel as they had not reached a verdict by the end of the first day of discussion. During this stay at the hotel, four members of the jury held a seance using a ouija board to try to contact the dead victims and ask who had killed them. The next day the jury returned a verdict of guilty. When the fact that the ouija board had been used became known, the defendant appealed and the Court of Appeal quashed the verdict and ordered a re-trial of the case.

Key Law

The court can inquire into what happened where the incident was not part of the jury discussions in the jury room.

 Sander v United Kingdom [2000] Crim LR 767

Key Facts

During the trial one juror wrote a note to the judge raising concern over the fact that other jurors had been openly making racist remarks and jokes. The judge asked the jury to 'search their consciences'. The next day the judge received two letters, one signed by all the jurors (including the juror who had made the complaint) in which they denied any racist attitudes and a second from one juror who admitted that he may have been the one making racist jokes. Despite the discrepancy between the two letters, the judge allowed the case to continue. The ECHR held that in these circumstances the judge should have discharged the jury as there was an obvious risk of racial bias.

Key Law

Where the judge is alerted to an obvious risk of racial bias before the trial ends then he has power to discharge the jury.

R v Connor: R v Mirza (conjoined appeals) [2004] UKHL 4

R v Connor

Key Facts

The two defendants were jointly charged with wounding. They were both convicted by a majority verdict of 10–2. Five days after the verdict (but before sentence was passed) one of the jurors wrote to the Crown Court stating that while many jurors thought it was one or other of the defendants who had committed the stabbing, they would convict both to 'teach them a lesson'. The complaining juror said that, when she argued that the jury should consider which defendant was responsible, her co-jurors had refused to listen and remarked that if they did that they could be a week considering verdicts in the case.

R v Mirza

Key Facts

The defendant was a Pakistani who settled in the UK in 1988. He had an interpreter to help him in the trial and during the trial the jury sent notes asking why he needed an interpreter. He was convicted on a 10–2 majority. Six days after the jury verdict, one juror wrote to the defendant's counsel alleging that from the start of the trial there had been a 'theory' that the use of an interpreter was a 'ploy'. The juror also said that she had been shouted down when she objected and reminded her fellow jurors of the judge's directions.

Key Law

The common law rule which protected jurors' confidentiality and which precluded the court from admitting evidence of what had happened in the jury room after the verdict had been given is still effective. This rule is compatible with Art 6 of the European Convention on Human Rights.

R v Karakaya [2005] EWCA Crim 346

 Key Facts

A juror did an internet search and brought the information into the jury room during deliberations following an overnight adjournment. The print outs were discovered by the jury bailiff. D's conviction was quashed as being unsafe.

 Key Law

This contravened the fundamental rule that no evidence was to be introduced after the jury had retired to consider their verdict.

 Key Link

R v Gearing [1968] 1 WLR 344.

7.5 Contempt of court

 Attorney General v Associated Newspapers [1994] 1 All ER 556

 Key Facts

The *Mail on Sunday* published details of the jury's deliberations in the Blue Arrow fraud case. The information had been obtained from two members of the jury by an independent researcher who later gave transcripts of the interviews to a journalist. The convictions of the newspaper, its editor and the journalist concerned, under s 8 of the Contempt of Court Act 1981 were upheld by the House of Lords.

 Key Law

The word 'disclose' in s 8 applies to both the revelation of deliberations by jurors and any further disclosure by publication. It does not matter that the information of what happened in the jury room has come indirectly through another person.

 Attorney General v Scotcher [2005] UKHL 36

 Key Facts

A juror who wrote to the two defendants' mother after the jury verdict, disclosing their deliberations and expressing views as to the unsatisfactory nature of the jury discussion, was in contempt under s 8 of the Contempt of Court Act 1981.

Key Law

Section 8 of the Contempt of Court Act 1981 does not allow disclosure to a third party, even if D has a genuine belief that there has been a miscarriage of justice.

Key Comment

The Court of Appeal pointed out that D could have written to the judge or the Court of Appeal expressing his concerns.

Lay Magistrates

Anonymity of magistrates

R v Felixstowe Justices, ex p Leigh (1987)
Open justice demands that the names of those who sit in judgment should be known

No bias

R v Sussex Justices, ex p McCarthy (1924)
There must not be even a suspicion that there has been an improper interference with the course of justice

Lay Magistrates

Role of the clerk

R v Eccles Justices, ex p Fitzpatrick (1989)
A clerk should not retire with justices as a matter of course

Practice Direction (2000)
Justices should seek the advice of the clerk in open court

8.1 Anonymity of magistrates

(DC) R v Felixstowe Justices, ex p Leigh [1987] 1 All ER 551

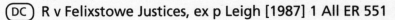

Key Facts

A bench of magistrates had a policy of withholding the names of justices, both during the hearing of a case and afterwards. A journalist reporting a case asked for the names of the bench but was refused. That journalist successfully applied for an order directing the clerk to disclose the identities of the bench and also for a declaration that the bench's policy of non-disclosure was unlawful.

Key Law

(1) The practice of claiming anonymity when sitting as a magistrate is unlawful.
(2) Open justice demands that the names of those who sit in judgment should be known.

Key Judgment: Watkins LJ

'It is an occupational hazard that magistrates and other judges should accept, that they will occasionally be subjected to criticism, and even vilification, and that they will be pestered by persons who bear some grudge.'

8.2 No bias

(DC) **R v Sussex Justices, ex p McCarthy [1924] 1 KB 256**

Key Facts

Following a road traffic accident, McCarthy (M) was summonsed for dangerous driving. At the end of the case, when the magistrates retired to consider their verdict, the clerk of the court went with them. M was found guilty. His lawyers then discovered that the clerk was a partner in a firm of solicitors that was acting in a civil claim for a person who had been injured in the accident. There was no evidence that the clerk had in any way influenced the decision, but M's lawyers successfully applied to the Divisional Court for the conviction to be quashed.

Key Law

Nothing should be done which creates even a suspicion that there has been an improper interference with the course of justice.

Key Judgment: Lord Hewart CJ

'It is of fundamental importance that justice should not only be done but manifestly and undoubtedly be seen to be done.'

8.3 Role of the clerk

 R v Eccles Justices, ex p Fitzpatrick (1989)
89 Cr App Rep 324

 Key Facts

Fitzpatrick (F) was charged with burglary. He had elected summary trial and pleaded not guilty. He then sought to change his plea. During the hearing for this, the clerk of the court took an active role and retired with the magistrates when they considered the request. F was allowed to change his plea and the magistrates then heard mitigation in respect of sentencing. When they retired to consider the sentence, they asked the clerk to retire with them. He did so and remained with them for most of the time. The magistrate decided to commit F to the Crown Court for sentence. The Divisional Court quashed this decision and sent the case back to the Magistrates' court to be reheard by a new bench with a different clerk.

 Key Facts

(1) Any request to the clerk to accompany the justices when they retire to consider a case should be made clearly by the magistrates and in open court.

(2) A clerk should not retire with justices as a matter of course.

 Key Comment

With the implementation of the Human Rights Act 1998, this point has now been made even clearer in the following Practice Direction.

Practice Direction [2000] 4 All ER 895

Para 8

'At any time justices are entitled to receive advice to assist them in discharging their responsibilities. If they are in doubt as to the evidence which has been given, they should seek the aid of their legal adviser, referring to his/her notes as appropriate. This should normally be done in open court. Where the justices request their adviser to join them in the retiring room, this request should be made in the presence of the parties in court. Any legal advice given to the justices other than in open court should be clearly stated to be provisional and the adviser should subsequently repeat the substance of the advice in open court and give the parties an opportunity to make any representations they wish on that professional advice. The legal adviser should then state in open court whether the professional advice is confirmed or, if it is varied, the nature of the variation.'

9

Civil Courts and Procedure

Civil Procedure

Rules
Rule 1.1(1)
The overriding objective is to enable the court to deal with cases justly

Rule 1.4
The court must further the overriding objective by actively managing cases

Timetables

Vinos v Marks & Spencer plc (2001)
Time limits set out in the CPR are to be strictly observed

Godwin v Swindon Borough Council (2001)
The deemed day of service was not rebuttable by evidence showing that service had actually been effected in time

Civil Courts and Procedure

Encouraging ADR

Scott v Avery (1856)
If there is an agreement to arbitrate, court proceedings will be stayed

Cable & Wireless plc v IBM (2002)
A specific clause agreeing to go to ADR is enforceable

R (Cowl) v Plymouth City Council (2001)
Lawyers are under a duty to resort to litigation only as a last resort

Dunnett v Railtrack plc (2002)
Failure to use ADR can lead to cost penalties

Halsey v Milton Keynes General NHS Trust (2004)
Costs normally follow the event but unreasonable refusal to try ADR can lead to departure from this rule

Burchell v Bullard (2005)
The parties cannot ignore a proper request to mediate simply because it was made before the claim was issued

Earl of Malmesbury v Strutt and Parker (2008)
Taking an unreasonable position in mediation so that it fails can result in a costs penalty

9.1 Overriding objective

Civil Procedure Rules

Rule 1.1(1)
'These rules are a new procedural code with the overriding objective of enabling the court to deal with cases justly.'

Civil Procedure Rules

Rule 1.2
'Dealing with a case justly includes, so far as practicable:

(a) ensuring that the parties are on an equal footing;
(b) saving expense;
(c) dealing with the case in ways which are proportionate to:
   (i)   the amount of money involved;
   (ii) the importance of the case;
   (iii) the complexity of the issues; and
   (iv) the financial position of each party;
(d) ensuring that it is dealt with expeditiously and fairly; and
(e) allotting to it an appropriate share of the court's resources, while taking into account the need to allot resources to other cases.'

9.2 Case management

Civil Procedure Rules

Rule 1.4
'(1) The court must further the overriding objective by actively managing cases.

(2) Active case management includes:

(a) encouraging the parties to co-operate with each other in the conduct of the proceedings;
(b) identifying the issues at an early stage;
(c) deciding promptly which issues need full investigation and trial and accordingly disposing summarily of the others;
(d) deciding the order in which issues are to be decided;
(e) encouraging the parties to use an alternative dispute resolution procedure if the court considers that appropriate and facilitating the use of such procedure;

(f) helping the parties settle the whole or part of the case;

(g) fixing timetables or otherwise controlling the progress of the case;

(h) considering whether the likely benefit of taking a particular step justify the cost of taking it;

(i) dealing with the case without the parties needing to attend court;

(j) making use of technology; and

(k) giving directions to ensure that the trial of a case proceeds quickly and efficiently.'

9.2.1 Encouraging ADR

(HL) **Scott v Avery (1856) 5 HL Cas 811**

Key Facts

Insurance policies in respect of a ship included clauses that stated (1) that any 'difference' should be referred to arbitration and (2) that any party who refused to refer the matter to arbitration could not bring or continue a claim on the policy in the courts. One party brought a court action, but the court held that such clauses were lawful and stayed the case.

Key Law

Where there is an agreement to go to arbitration, any court proceedings will be stayed.

(HC) **Cable & Wireless plc v IBM [2002] EWHC 2059 Comm**

Key Facts

The parties had an agreement under which IBM was to supply information technology. In the event of a dispute, the agreement contained the following clause:

> 'If the matter is not resolved by negotiation, the parties shall attempt in good faith to resolve the dispute or claim through an Alternative Dispute Resolution (ADR) procedure as recommended to the parties by the Centre for Dispute Resolution. However, an ADR procedure which is being followed shall not prevent any party from issuing proceedings.'

A dispute arose and the claimants issued proceedings and refused to go through any ADR procedure. The judge held the clause was enforceable and stayed the proceedings for ADR to be attempted.

Key Law

A clause in an agreement to go to ADR in the event of a dispute can be binding on the parties. The clause must be more than an agreement to negotiate.

 R (Cowl) v Plymouth City Council [2001] EWCA Civ 1935, [2002] 1 WLR 803

Key Facts

Plymouth City Council decided to close a care home. Six of the residents at the home applied for judicial review of the decision. This application was dismissed. On the residents' appeal against that dismissal, the Court of Appeal stated *obiter* that ADR should be considered even where one of the parties was a public body.

Key Law

(1) The court is entitled of its own initiative to enquire into why some form of ADR has not been used to resolve or reduce the issues in dispute.

(2) Lawyers are under a duty to resort to litigation only as a last resort. ADR should be used in suitable cases.

 Dunnett v Railtrack plc [2002] EWCA Civ 303, [2002] 2 All ER 850

Key Facts

Following judgment in favour of the claimant, the judge granted Ds leave to appeal, but urged them to try ADR rather than use the appeal process. Ds refused to try ADR. Their appeal was successful, but the Court of Appeal refused to grant them their costs because of their refusal to consider using ADR.

Key Law

Failure to use ADR can lead to cost penalties.

Key Judgment: Brooke LJ

'Schooled mediators are now able to achieve results satisfactory to both parties in many cases which are quite beyond the power of lawyers and courts to achieve.'

Halsey v Milton Keynes General NHS Trust [2004] EWCA Civ 576

 Key Facts

This involved a claim for clinical negligence which it was alleged caused the death of the claimant's husband. C's solicitors repeatedly invited Ds to submit the matter to mediation. Ds repeatedly refused, as they correctly predicted that they were not liable. The claimant argued that even though she had lost the appeal, she should not be ordered to pay all Ds' costs because of their refusal to mediate. The Court of Appeal granted Ds' costs but laid down general principles on when cost penalties should be incurred.

 Key Law

(1) Costs normally follow the event. To depart from this rule it must be shown that the successful party acted unreasonably in refusing to agree to the use of ADR.

(2) Factors to be taken into account in deciding whether the rejection of ADR is unreasonable include:
- the nature of the dispute;
- the merits of the case;
- the extent to which other settlement methods have been attempted;
- whether the costs of the mediation would be disproportionately high;
- whether delay in setting up mediation would be prejudicial;
- whether the mediation had a reasonable prospect of success.

Burchell v Bullard [2005] EWCA Civ 358

 Key Facts

This involved a building dispute over an extension to Ds house. Prior to issuing proceedings, C proposed ADR but D refused to consider this. The court was asked to apply a costs penalty. The court found that the factors in Halsey (see above) were present but that they would not apply a costs penalty as the refusal to use ADR had occurred prior to the decisions in *Dunnett v Railtrack plc* (2002) and *Halsey v Milton Keynes General NHS Trust* (2004).

Key Law

The parties cannot ignore a proper request to mediate simply because it was made before the claim was issued.

Earl of Malmesbury v Strutt and Parker [2008] EWHC 424 (QB)

(HC)

Key Facts

The case involved negligence of estate agents who were acting on behalf of the claimant in negotiating leases for part of his land to Bournemouth Airport. The claim was for just over £87 million. Mediation was attempted but the claimant's solicitors approached the mediation with a very high figure in mind and refused to move from this during the course of the mediation. The mediation failed. When the case was tried, the claimant won but was awarded only just under £1 million. The judge held that position taken by the claimant's side during mediation was unreasonable and only awarded the claimant a small amount of his costs.

Key Law

A party who agrees to mediation but then causes the mediation to fail because of his unreasonable position in the mediation is, in reality, in the same position as a party who has unreasonably refused to mediate.

9.2.2 Timetables

(CA) Vinos v Marks & Spencer plc [2001] 3 All ER 784

Key Facts

The claimant (V) had suffered injuries at work. After lengthy attempts to negotiate a settlement failed, V's solicitors issued court proceedings one week before the expiry of the limitation period. They did not serve these proceedings on D until nine days after the end of the four-month period set down in the Civil Procedure Rules. They applied for an extension of time. The court refused the extension.

Key Law

Time limits set out in the CPR are to be strictly observed.

Key Comment

The court refused to apply CPR 7.6 as it only allows for an extension if:

(a) the court has been unable to serve the claim form; or
(b) the claimant has taken all reasonable steps to serve the claim form but has been unable to do so; and
(c) in either case the claimant has acted promptly in making the application.

None of these applied in the *Vinos* case.

The court also refused to use CPR 3.10 which gives the court a general power to remedy an error of procedure. It was not appropriate as it would be in contradiction to the specific rule in CPR 7.6(3).

 ## Godwin v Swindon Borough Council [2001] EWCA Civ 1478, [2001] 4 All ER 641

 Key Facts

A claim form arrived at the defendant's address for service within the time limit. However, because of a 'deeming' provision in CPR 6.7(1) it was deemed to have arrived three days late. The court held that service was out of time.

 Key Law

The deemed day of service was not rebuttable by evidence showing that service had actually been effected in time.

 Key Link

Anderton v Clwyd County Council [2002] EWCA Civ 933, [2002] 3 All ER 813.

10

Police Powers

Stop/search

Osman v DPP (1999)
Police must comply with requirements of s 1 PACE or else their use of stop and search powers are unlawful

Gillan and Quinton v UK (2010)
Powers to stop and search under s 44 Terrorism Act 2000 are too wide and breach human rights

Searching premises

R v Longman (1988)
Police may use force or subterfuge to gain entry to premises under a warrant

O'Loughlin v Chief Constable of Essex (1998)
Police should give reasons at point of entry unless it is impracticable

Powers of arrest

R v Self (1992)
If D has not committed an arrestable offence then an arrest by a private citizen is unlawful

Taylor v Chief Constable of Thames Valley Police (2004)
The person arrested must be told the reason for arrest in simple language

Police Powers

Powers of detention

R v Samuel (1988)
D must have access to a lawyer unless it is one of the situations set out in PACE where access can be delayed

R v Aspinall (1999)
A vulnerable person must have an appropriate adult present during police interviews

Charles v Crown Prosecution Service (2009)
D cannot normally be interviewed after he has been told he will be charged

Samples

S and Marper v United Kingdom (2009)
Indefinite retention of DNA records is a breach of human rights

10.1 Powers to stop and search

 Osman v DPP (1999) The Times, 28 September

 Key Facts

Police officers failed to give their names or station when using their powers of stop and search. This made the search unlawful.

O had resisted the search and been charged with assaulting a police officer in the execution of duty. Because the search was unlawful O was entitled to use reasonable force.

Key Law

Police officers must comply with the requirements in s 1 Police and Criminal Evidence Act 1984 (PACE). If they do not, then the use of the power to stop and search is unlawful.

➡ **Key Link**

Michaels v Highbury Corner Magistrates' Court [2009] EWHC 2928 (Admin)

ECHR Gillan v United Kingdom: Quinton v United Kingdom [2010] Crim LR 415

 Key Facts

The applicants were, in separate instances, stopped and searched under the powers given by s 44 of the Terrorism Act 2000. They were then allowed to go on their way. They complained that s 44 breached their rights under various Articles of the European Convention on Human Rights. These were Articles 5 (right to liberty), 8 (right to respect for private life), 10 (freedom of expression) and 11 (freedom of assembly and association). The European Court of Human Rights held that s 44 breached Article 8. The court made no finding on any of the other Articles.

Key Law

Section 44 of the Terrorism Act 2000 breach Article 8 of the European Convention on Human Rights because it did not require the stop and search to be 'necessary' only 'expedient'. The discretion conferred on individual police officers was too broad. Also the fact that it was unnecessary for an officer to demonstrate the existence of any reasonable suspicion or have any subjective suspicion made the section too wide.

There was also a risk that such a widely framed power could be misused against demonstrators and protestors in breach of Articles 10 and/or 11.

10.2 Power to enter and search premises

 CA R v Longman [1988] Crim LR 534

 Key Facts

The police had a warrant to search specific premises. They knew that it would be difficult to gain entry, so they arranged for a plain clothes police woman to pretend to be delivering flowers from Interflora. When the door was opened to her, the police burst into the premises without immediately identifying themselves or showing the search warrant. Once in the property they showed the search warrant. It was held that the search was lawful.

 Key Law

Where police have a warrant to search premises, they may use force or subterfuge to gain entry. The warrant should be shown to the occupiers as soon as reasonably practical.

 CA O'Loughlin v Chief Constable of Essex [1998] 1 WLR 374

 Key Facts

Police forced their way into premises without explaining that it was in order to arrest O'Loughlin's wife for criminal damage. This made the entry unlawful and O'Loughlin was successful in claiming damages for injuries sustained when he tried to prevent the police from entering.

 Key Law

Police should give reasons for entry unless the circumstances make it impracticable.

 Key Judgment: Buxton LJ

'Freedom of the home from invasion is an interest of comparable importance to freedom from arrest and is deserving of a comparable degree of protection.'

10.3 Powers of arrest

 R v Self [1992] 3 All ER 476

 Key Facts

A store detective arrested Self (S) because he thought that S had stolen a bar of chocolate. S resisted the arrest and assaulted the detective. S was acquitted of theft but convicted of assault. On appeal it was held that as S had been acquitted of theft there was no arrestable offence and the arrest by the detective was unlawful. This meant that S was entitled to use reasonable force to free himself and so his conviction for assault was quashed.

 Key Law

The power of private citizens to arrest is more limited than police officers. Where D had not committed an arrestable offence then a private citizen did not have power to arrest, even though there was reasonable suspicion that D had committed an arrestable offence.

 Key Comment

Since the decision in *Self* the law on powers of arrest has changed. It is now governed by s 24A of PACE (a new section inserted by s 110 of the Serious Organised Crime and Police Act 2005). Section 24A limits arrest by private citizens to indictable offences instead of arrestable offences. The arrest can be made if someone is in the act of committing an indictable offence or where the citizen has reasonable grounds for suspecting the person to be committing an indictable offence. An arrest can also be made where there has been an indictable offence and there are reasonable grounds for suspecting the person to be guilty of it. This keeps the same limitation that there must have been an offence committed, so the ruling in *Self* would still be the same.

 Taylor v Chief Constable of Thames Valley Police [2004] EWCA Civ 1022

 Key Facts

Taylor was a 10-year-old boy who had been throwing stones during an anti-vivisection demo. When he was present at a later protest he was identified by a police officer who arrested him saying: 'I am arresting you on suspicion of violent disorder on April 18, 1998 at Hillgrove Farm.' He sued for unlawful arrest, but the Court of Appeal held that it was a lawful arrest.

Key Law

The person arrested must be told in simple, non-technical language that they can understand the essential legal and factual grounds for their arrest.

10.4 Powers of detention

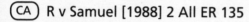

(CA) R v Samuel [1988] 2 All ER 135

Key Facts

Samuel (S) was arrested on suspicion of robbery. His mother was informed of his arrest but when, during an interview by the police, S asked for a solicitor, the police refused him access to any lawyer. Shortly after, S confessed to the robbery. At his trial S contended that the evidence of his confession should be excluded as he had been refused access to legal advice. He was convicted. The conviction was quashed.

Key Law

PACE clearly sets out that access to legal advice can only be refused where the police believe that allowing consultation with a solicitor will lead to interference with, or harm to, the evidence or to other people, alert others or hinder the recovery of property.

Key Comment

This case stresses the importance of the right of access to legal advice.

(CA) R v Aspinall [1999] 2 Cr App Rep 115,

Key Facts

Aspinall (A) was arrested and taken to a police station. A police surgeon examined him and noted that he was a schizophrenic and on regular medication. The surgeon noted that A was anxious but lucid and probably fit to be interviewed. By the time of his interview A had been in custody some 13 hours. He initially requested a solicitor but changed his mind and stated he was anxious to get home to his family. Evidence of the interview was excluded, as it was held there should have been an appropriate adult present at the interview. Because of his mental illness A was a vulnerable person.

Key Law

Vulnerable people should have an appropriate adult present during police interviews.

 Charles v Crown Prosecution Service [2009] EWHC 3521 (Admin)

Key Facts

D was found slumped over the steering wheel of a car and was arrested for being in charge of a vehicle whilst under the influence of drink or drugs. He took a breath test and was informed that he would be charged. After this he was interviewed. He was not informed of the offence for which the police were investigating him at the start of the interview. He was then charged with driving whilst under the influence of drink or drugs. The magistrates allowed the statement taken from him in the interview to be used in evidence. His conviction was quashed as there had been a breach of the Code of Practice in interviewing D.

Key Law

The Code of Practice under PACE stated that:

> *'a detainee may not be interviewed about an offence after they have been charged with, or informed that they may be prosecuted for it, unless the interview is necessary'.*

These provisions are designed to protect a detainee and cannot be ignored.

10.5 Taking of samples

 S v United Kingdom: Marper v United Kingdom [2009] Crim LR 355

Key Facts

S, aged 11, had been found not guilty of attempted robbery. M had been charged with harassment of his partner but the case had been dropped. Both had had DNA samples taken and their DNA profiles had been retained on the national police database. Both argued that the retention of their records on the database was contrary to their right to respect for private and family life under Article 8(1) of the

European Convention on Human Rights. The European Court of Human Rights held that there was a breach of Article 8.

 Key Law

The indefinite retention of DNA records of those who were not convicted of an offence was a breach of their right to respect for private life.

11

Criminal Courts and Procedure

11.1 Overriding objective

Rule 1.1 of the Criminal Procedure Rules states:

'(1) The overriding objective of this new code is that criminal cases be dealt with justly.

(2) Dealing with a criminal case justly includes:

   (a) acquitting the innocent and convicting the guilty;

   (b) dealing with the prosecution and the defence fairly;

   (c) recognising the rights of a defendant, particularly those under Article 6 of the European Convention on Human Rights;

   (d) respecting the interests of witnesses, victims and jurors and keeping them informed of the progress of the case;

   (e) dealing with the case efficiently and expeditiously;

   (f) ensuring that appropriate information is available to the court when bail and sentence are considered; and

   (g) dealing with the case in ways that take into account:

      (i)   the gravity of the offence alleged,

      (ii)   the complexity of what is in issue,

      (iii)   the severity of the consequences for the defendant and others affected, and

      (iv)   the needs of other cases.'

11.2 Active case management

Rule 3.2 of the Criminal Procedure Rules states:

'(1) The court must further the overriding objective by actively managing the case.

(2) Active case management includes:

   (a) the early identification of the real issues;

   (b) the early identification of the needs of witnesses;

(c) achieving a certainty as to what must be done, by whom, and when, in particular by the early setting of a timetable for the progress of a case;

(d) monitoring the progress of the case and compliance with directions;

(e) ensuring that the evidence, whether disputed or not, is presented in the shortest and clearest way;

(f) discouraging delay, dealing with as many aspects of the case as possible on the same occasion, and avoiding unnecessary hearings;

(g) encouraging the participants to co-operate in the progression of the case; and

(h) making use of technology.'

Index